ISLAM AND GOD-CENTRICITY: A THEOLOGICAL BASIS FOR HUMAN LIBERATION

by

Shaykh Arif Abdul Hussain

Printed in the United Kingdom.

ISBN 978-1-9998621-1-4

Published by:
Sajjadiyya Press, 60 Weoley Park Road,
Selly Oak, Birmingham, B29 6RB

Author: Shaykh Arif Abdul Hussain

CONTENTS

ACKNOWLEDGEMENTS v

NIGHT ONE 1

NIGHT TWO 18

NIGHT THREE 32

NIGHT FOUR 46

NIGHT FIVE 52

NIGHT SIX 66

NIGHT SEVEN 75

NIGHT EIGHT 88

NIGHT NINE 97

NIGHT TEN 103

NIGHT ELEVEN 119

ACKNOWLEDGEMENTS

THE FOLLOWING LECTURES were delivered at the Hyderi Islamic centre on the first eleven nights of Muharram 1437 (October 2015). The author wishes to express his sincere gratitude to the community for their appreciation of these talks and especially wishes to thank Sarfaraz Jeraj and Abbas Datoo for their cordial invitation and hospitality. While every attempt has been made to preserve the original content of these lectures, some changes have been inevitable to accommodate for the written word.

Night One

I would like to begin by thanking you for giving me this opportunity to address you and to be here to receive the blessings that come with the remembrance of Imam Ḥusayn. We thank Allah for keeping us alive to witness this occasion once again, for allowing us to revive our faith and to bring about that beautiful transformation that needs to be brought about through the remembrance of Ḥusayn ibn ʿAlī. This transformation is one whereby mere mortals are turned into human beings in the truest sense of what it means to be human, such that they begin to resemble the glorious ranks of the angels by allowing the true angelic beauty that is within us to emerge and manifest itself. Indeed, Imam Ḥusayn has brought about such a phenomenal reform within the human community that not only the faith of Islam but humanity as a whole is indebted to him. He revives the spirit of humanity, restores its dignity, and gives a glimpse of the loftiest status awaiting us so that humanity itself reaches the threshold of divinity, and begins to resemble the Most Beautiful.

Imam Khomeini, in one of his lectures on Hajj, says that if the powers of the world were to spend their entire treasure in creating a platform to gather people to impart a single message they would not be able to do so, yet the platform created by Hajj is one that people flock to. I will say similarly that the platform created by Imam Ḥusayn through the sincerity of his devotion to Allah and what he offered on the day of Ashura (the 10th day of Muharram) is one that goes beyond Karbala and spreads across the entire Earth. He commands the respect of minds all over the world and transcends colours and religions. We see this so clearly within Africa and India: when it comes to Ḥusayn ibn ʿAlī people go beyond their persuasions and say, "Indeed we relate to him." This platform that Imam Ḥusayn has created for us is thus a platform through which the whole of the Muslim community can be reformed. People from all walks of life come together diligently for ten days and learn from the supreme sacrifice of Imam Ḥusayn. For ten days, their minds and hearts are open to receiving his message, they are willing to learn from him so that they may make something of their lives and in order to bring about much needed goodness in this world of ours.

Before I commence with the topic, it is worthy of mention that Imam Ḥusayn was extremely spiritual. In those few hours of Ḥusayn ibn ʿAlī's life that we know, he has impacted us to the core. Have we ever seen a person who has only been studied for a few hours of his life but in himself becomes a religion and an institution? This is not merely an emotional attachment – there are gems of humanity that he displayed in those few hours. There are moral, spiritual and social lessons we can learn through the story of the Imam. A story of integrity, dignity, courage, righteousness, morality, spirituality, and of how to grow in the face of what seems to be an apparent defeat; of how to allow suffering to work positively in the development of the human soul. Have we ever seen a person who, at the decapitation of his son, becomes even more spiritual? Have we ever seen a person who eulogises Allah even more when he is thirsty than he was before encountering the thirst? Have we ever seen a person being struck with swords, spears, arrows, stones, and yet his lips move in supplication to Allah even more intensely than they were before he was attacked? Have we ever seen a person who has fallen from his steed, who, at the point of death, his face begins to radiate with such beauty and with such serenity that even his antagonists are moved by it? Where have we ever seen a man regarding whom even the people filled with hatred towards him, people the likes of whom Allah says, "Your hearts became as hard as rocks, or even harder [...]" (2:74), themselves being moved when they encounter the serenity of Ḥusayn ibn ʿAlī, the very man they have set out to murder? This man is truly a man that strikes at the heart of humanity. He is beyond persuasions, colours, cultures, religions; beyond time and space even.

So, I ask you, has there ever been such a universal figure within the folds of humanity who impacts people as profoundly as Ḥusayn ibn ʿAlī, even though for the majority of us, all we know about him are some meagre six hours of his life? What this fact reveals to us is that this man is immersed in God to the level that he becomes Godly. Just as God is colourless and directionless, this man of His, this devotee of His, who gives himself to the blade and sacrifices everything else he possesses, becomes as colourless, directionless, statusless and without denomination as God. In his colourlessness he encompasses all colours. In his being without direction, every direction tends to him. In his being statusless, every status calls out for him. In his having no language, every language proclaims him. Every heart beats with that name regardless of whether they acknowledge him as Ḥusayn, or as Shabīr, or by any other name. How wonderful is this man, and how profound is the impact that he has made upon us. So I shall say, not only the faith of Islam but humanity at large is indebted to him. It is not an exaggeration that the poets recite that the whole of the prophetic mission culminates in his sacrifice. That if righteousness has ever had a standard – an absolute standard – it is him: Ḥusayn ibn ʿAlī.

I will narrate this incident as I begin my topic. Somebody called me many years ago and she said, "Can you perform my divorce?" I said, "Well I have to know which school of thought you belong to." She replied, "I don't know." I said, "In that case tell me, after the Prophet who is the successor?" She said, "I don't know." So I asked her, "Do you know Imam ʿAlī?" She said "No." I said, "Caliph Abū Bakr?" She said, "No". I said, "Caliph ʿUmar?" She said "No". I said, "Well, what other personality do you recognise apart from the Prophet?" She said, "The only other name I recognise is Imam Ḥusayn." This is how this man has impacted the minds and the hearts. If we take away the label of "Shīʿa," he becomes the heritage of the Ummah at large. If we take away the label of "Islam," he becomes the heritage of humanity at large. Look at the camp that is with him: slaves, black, white, Muslims, non-Muslims, men, women, old, young – and all of them relate to him equally. This is how broad this man is.

We take great pride in Ḥusayn ibn ʿAlī, a man whose humanity can culminate in such glory and can stand at such peaks that when everything is taken away from him his dignity remains intact, his morals are impeccable, his spirituality is ascending. Imagine this of Ḥusayn: as he is being cut into pieces and his eyes are tearing, his men ask him, "Ḥusayn, why do you tear? You are the bravest upon the face of the Earth and amongst the chosen ones of God".

He says, "These tears are for those who kill me."

"Why do you weep for them, O Ḥusayn?"

"At their fate that awaits them. My heart breaks that these souls have wasted themselves and Allah has made me a test for them. Through me they will incur damnation, and that is what breaks my heart." At the peak of battle, this is what his heart feels for his enemy.

Our topic "Islam, God-Centricity and Human Liberation" is aptly attributed to Imam Ḥusayn. "Islam" means submission and wholesome surrender to Allah. "God-centricity," the highest principle, means that everything within human life is focused specifically towards Allah, the point of absolute perfection. As for "human liberation," what we mean by this is having a system which allows humanity – all of humanity – to arrive at the lofty pedestals it is destined for. There was a reason why the angels were commanded to prostrate before Adam. Adam and his children are destined to reach certain glorious heights, heights that can only be achieved through a process of liberation. This process of liberation can only come about if humanity is focused on Allah and directed towards Him. This focus towards Allah can only come about through a wholesome surrender to Allah which is beyond any restraints. Thus it is apt to connect Islam in the truest meaning of this word to Ḥusayn ibn ʿAlī; the Islam of Ḥusayn was *absolute* surrender. The focus of Ḥusayn towards Allah is witnessed when his son ʿAlī Akbar falls in front him. Ḥusayn weeps and says, "O child, your death tears your father's arteries apart, but it becomes easier through the knowledge that Allah witnesses what they have done to you and preserves the souls with what they have done." The focus that Imam Ḥusayn had, the God-centricity, when he falls and says, "O Lord, grand are You in Your ranks, lofty is Your majesty, near in proximity You are, You respond to every supplication." Such are his focus and personal liberation that even at the killings of his beloved brother ʿAbbās, his sons Akbar and Asghar, he does not lose his sense of righteousness and his morality.

As human beings it is essential that we understand the world, the nature of our lives, and have some notion as to what we are all about. Only then can we live a meaningful life. When a human being awakens in this world and sees natural phenomena he feels a need to make sense of it, because a human being cannot exist in isolation of feeling in control. This control for human beings is brought about through knowledge of what is happening around them. When human beings in the past observed the Sun rise in the day and set at night, they connected human life and the fate of humanity to the rising and setting of the Sun, and as a result they viewed the setting of the Sun as a frightful event for them. They constructed a worldview which led them to believe that the Sun is their God, and hence at night they would offer devotion to the Sun to ensure that it would rise again the next morning. This was the worldview in which they lived. But it was a restrictive worldview.

At every point in our history human beings have tried to make sense of the world and gain an understanding of all its interconnections in order to lead a meaningful life. Whatever we understand of our world informs our attitudes – our interpretation of the events of this world, our appreciation of this world and this will inevitably have a bearing on our level of growth. So, for example (and I often give this example, but it is a befitting one so I will give it again), at one point in our history the world was thought to be flat. This belief not only informed people as to how they should look at the world, but to some extent it also curtailed them. It informed them in the sense that it allowed them to interpret the rest of the universe and the celestial bodies in a way which accorded with their understanding that the Earth was flat, while on the other hand it curtailed them as to how far they would go in exploring this world. Their belief prompted them to create crafts and traverse the seas, but curtailed them in making smaller crafts because if they were to set sail there is a possibility, they thought, that the ocean might end, and they might fall over the edge due to the Earth being flat. It informed them not only in terms of how they understood the world, but also how their activities ought to be carried out. It guided them insofar as they would think twice about how much they should aspire and where they should and should not venture. This is how the relationship between the world and the human mind has always been. The human mind first needs to make sense of the world and then that understanding subsequently determines how much they will strive, to what extent they will evolve, and how much they shall develop.

Now, let us look at the historical development of worldviews and paradigms, the astronomical one, let us say, the cosmological ones. At one point we used to operate on the Aristotelian paradigm that the Earth was the centre of the universe and that everything else was a weightless body in the sky. We used to believe that everything was determined. This cosmological worldview persisted for many centuries and influenced the way human beings thought of themselves and the world about them. Because of this, the Christians constructed a whole theology of the supremacy of human beings based upon the centrality of the Earth. They said, "Earth is the centre of the universe. This therefore proves that everything is created in honour of the Earth, and the most superior being on the face of the Earth is the human being, and therefore the centrality of the Earth is an indication of the supremacy of human beings.

And that supremacy is a God-given supremacy." As soon as it was discovered that the Earth was not the centre of the universe but was just as meaningless as any other celestial body, of which we now know there are trillions, the notion that the Earth is at the centre of the universe and therefore indicative of the supremacy of human beings also became meaningless. When the previous theological understanding of the universe was shown to be false, with it went the claim — to some extent at least — that the teachings of Christianity were founded on divine foreknowledge. And of course, in its place a whole awakening came about: the industrial revolution, the growth of the scientific mind, with religious power and authority diminishing. So the worldview informs us how to think and how to understand things.

Let me give you another example. If we were to say that the Earth is flat then we would conclude, legally within Islam, that there must be only one first day of the lunar month across the entire globe because as soon as the moon arrives into the horizon, it is one moon that the *whole* Earth should potentially see at one and the same time. How we think the world is therefore informs our legal interpretations of *fiqh*. Our worldviews are such that they allow us to construct the rest of our world around that worldview.

By the seventeenth century, the principle of gravity which Newton discovered challenged the older Aristotelian understanding of the universe. Newton showed that the universe was mechanistic and that everything observes fixed laws. Through his discovery of the laws of gravitation, Newton demonstrated that gravity is the force that pulls things to the Earth. He allegedly observed the apple falling upon his head, and began to think why did the apple fall? Why did it not go sideways, why did it not rise, why does everything fall? And from such observations he deduced that there is something like gravity. And through that he constructed a worldview that every part of the universe can be predicted accurately, and if we can understand this principle of gravity, it can work for us. Through this principle we were able to send probes to the Moon and to Mars. The problem after Newton was that newer findings about the universe and its working were not falling neatly within the system he created. So what did we do? We cut, we chopped, and we forced them to fit within the Newtonian paradigm until it became so overwhelmingly evident that the Newtonian paradigm is not quite accurate enough for understanding the wider universe. Then Einstein came with his theory of relativity, and a different theory of space emerged. At that point we said, "Yes, the laws of gravity which Newton discovered worked in part but cannot be used to interpret the workings of the wider physical universe. In other words, Newtonian physics was suitable for certain bodies within their own context; it had its place – but it does not work as far as the universe as a whole is concerned." So here our minds broadened: we were able to accurately interpret the new findings of physicists using the new paradigm put forward by Einstein. This is exactly what happens when we construct a worldview: it forces us to make sense of our religion, our morality and our understanding of society within that worldview.

Now, not only does the worldview influence the way in which we understand the rest of our lives and the way in which we behave, therefore, it also influences our notion of the afterlife. So, for example, the Pharaoh had this notion that the powerful on Earth would also be powerful in the afterlife. Therefore, according to his own worldview, at his death many of his slaves were killed and placed in the tomb with him, along with his riches of gold and diamonds. Because he would be a king in the afterlife and would need slaves and treasures in his new kingdom, ostentatious tombs were created for him. Our worldview informs not only how we behave in this world, how we treat the other, how we interpret our religion, how we make sense of our *fiqh*, how we make sense of morality, but it also determines the efforts we make for success in the afterlife.

Similarly, the notion that we are "the chosen ones" – the Jews of the past according to the Quran had this notion, and the Quran is replete with verses in which they say, "We are the sons of Allah," or, "We are the chosen ones" – what such belief does to us and to our minds is that it constructs a theology in which we are beyond reproach. No one can touch us or do anything to us. If you are the chosen one then any other being is dispensable: you can kill them, loot them, plunder them, leave them starving; you can usurp from them, and you will face no consequences. This is what the worldview does: it informs our morality, our actions to the fullest. The Quran narrates the Jews as having said that the *ummīyīn*, the gentiles, do not have any recourse to the Jewish people or any claim upon them. What they were saying was, "We are the chosen ones, we cannot be touched, we are the favoured ones of Allah," which is why they could lie and abuse the other. I am not saying that the Jews of today are like that, and I am not saying all Jews were alike. I am talking about the Jews that are mentioned in the verses of the Quran. The Quran is very open in condemning the Jews, but it is also open in condemning the Christians and Muslims; all three alike. It does not give immunity anyone.

On the other hand, imagine we had the belief which certain groups of Christians have that ʿĪsā (Jesus) has come and died for us and purged us of our sins. What does that do? It can give us a blanket permission to commit as many crimes as we want so long as we devote ourselves to ʿĪsā who has sacrificed himself and has absolved us of our sins. We are going to paradise so long as we believe in ʿĪsā and nothing else. In fact, many Shia groups have the belief that the love of Imam Ali will absolve them of all crimes however great or many. This is what the worldview does to us. If, furthermore, we have a particular worldview which says that everybody else is condemned and we are the only ones who are the chosen ones, then this immediately sets up a bias within our minds with regards to the other. Before the Prophet came to Medina, the Jews of Medina were warning the non-Jewish community that a Prophet will come, and when he came they would predominate. So when the Prophet began to preach in Mecca, the pagan chiefs warned the people to plug their ears by telling them the Prophet was a sorcerer, that he bewitched people and should not be believed. Nonetheless, overcome with curiosity the inhabitants of Medina, on their visit to Mecca, uncovered their ears and heard the verses of Sūrah al-Aʿrāf (Chapter of the Heights). Amazingly the content of these verses had nothing to do with Islam, but were actually providing the people with the Prophet's moral and spiritual worldview. In these verses he said, "O people, do not cheat each other. Do not bury your children. Do not sacrifice your children. Do not kill each other. Do not lie. Be good to each other." A man who was listening said: "He is talking about values that pertain to all of us but which all of us have forgotten. He is pointing out societal ills that are causing the devastation of the entire community." These were the most humanitarian verses ever to be revealed, agreed upon by all the Abrahamic faiths, agreed upon by every human being, and therefore those pagans agreed immediately that the Prophet's worldview makes sense. The correct paradigm is not one in which you should sacrifice for your gods to gain favours from them, nor one in which your gods will not sustain you until you sacrifice a child. It cannot be a right world in which you say that, "I can cheat the other, there's no consequence upon me because I am the chosen one." The Prophet's words made sense. So these inhabitants of Medina immediately said, "If this is the man that the Jews were talking about then this is the rightful Messenger of God; his paradigm works, his worldview is accurate."

But you know how the Jews of Medina reacted. They said, "He is a liar, he is copying everything from our scriptures, he has learnt it from us." Their reaction was similar to that of the disbelievers of Mecca who, being less sophisticated than them, levelled blames of sorcery against him: "He is a magician, he is a soothsayer, he learns from the Jews and the Christians." Their worldview, that they are the chosen ones, barred them from receiving the truth. The Prophet said, "There are no chosen ones – God does not have a chosen one." Instead the Quran says, "Truly those who do evil and are surrounded by their sins will be the inhabitants of the Fire, there to remain, while those who believe and do good deeds will be the inhabitants of the Garden, there to remain." (2:81-82) There is no chosen one in the book of God. But the Jews were adamant in their view: "We are the chosen ones, how dare he equate the pagans with us?" Their biases, their worldview, did not allow them to accept the Prophet nor to listen to what he was saying. On the other hand the pagans were open enough to listen to him and to say, "Actually, he is making a lot of sense. He has to be the Messenger because what he says makes sense to us." This is what our worldview does for us.

In Mecca, Islam was scattered amongst individuals, but in Medina it became the "religion of the state." It acquired social status, a social existence, and as a result the social norms, the laws, the do's and don'ts were revealed in Medina. This is amply clear in Sūra al-Baqara (Chapter of the Cow), which is filled with norms pertaining to societal affairs and human interactions. What's striking when we look at the first verses of this chapter is that it talks about the faithful as having belief in God, and after belief in God, as having certainty in the hereafter. We'll focus more on these two points later, but after that what do the verses say? "Who believe in everything revealed unto you (the Prophet) and everything revealed before you." (2:4) The Prophet's worldview was so broad that he said that the Muslim is someone who believes everything revealed in the Quran *and* whatever has been revealed in the Torah and the Bible, as well as the message brought by *all* the earlier Messengers. This was a very *broad* worldview which the Prophet presented, but the *biased* worldview of the Jews barred them from accepting it. What, then, do we mean by "Islam, God-centricity and Liberation"? Islam here is something that brings human beings to their natural condition. But what is the natural condition of humanity? Ever since the dawn of mankind, from Adam until our time, our natural condition has been one of constant evolution. We have been evolving, developing, maturing – that is the only thing we have been doing. Humanity was born in the cradle as an infant, as a baby. It learnt to crawl. It learnt to walk with the aid of a father holding its finger. It learnt to stand straight. It learnt to run, and to think and to continually evolve. That is what humanity has been doing from the stone ages to the present day in which we are conquering space. But this growth of humanity has been a very expensive one. It has not been an easy one. Humanity wants to evolve. It wants to burst forth because it is based on the principal of *lā ilāha illa Llāh*, "there is no god but God." *Lā ilāha* means there is no *false* god; it means there is nothing to restrain us. But then *illa Llāh* means the absolute completion. What we find is that at every moment human beings are moving continually forwards and then suddenly they are curtailed. They are not curtailed by anything except out-dated worldviews, either by way of religions, of cultures, of the cosmologies and paradigms they themselves have constructed but which are now the causes of their restriction and lack of growth and progression to the next stage of their evolution. What happens is that after a lot of struggle there is a break through that creates a broader worldview. It has come through revolutions, this growth. It has come through bloodshed, through calling people apostates and *kāfirs* (disbelievers), through burning them at the stake and crucifying them, killing them in their hundreds and thousands. It has been a very costly and expensive evolution and growth. But nonetheless, humanity has been on a unidirectional trend of growth.

What happens when an ovum is fertilized? It becomes a foetus and then takes birth as a baby. It crawls, it walks, it runs, it becomes a human being who is standing on his own feet. Then he begins to conquer the world through his intellect. And what happens at the end when the body starts to become frail and begins to descend to the Earth once again? The human being arrives at the noble, spiritual pedestal. We don't see a reverse trend; we are only seeing a unidirectional trend towards completion and growth. As soon as you bury a seed into the Earth it will sprout and start to grow again. From the big bang until now, if our appreciation of the physical five dimensions is accurate, what have we done in this universe? We have done nothing but grow and elaborate. This is the natural human condition – one of breaking all boundaries, all restraints, not curtailing itself at all. What Islam does for each and every one of us is that it informs us of *that* worldview of no restraints. It tells us that your grandfather was the one before whom the angels prostrated. It informs us that the heavens, the Sun, the Moon, the stars are all subservient to you. It tells us that God has created everything on this Earth for you. You don't need to prostrate to a rock or a stone anymore. You don't need to prostate before a star or a moon anymore. They are all *yours*. "O people, man and jinn, if you can penetrate within the realms of heavens then do so, you will not do so save by great force." (55:33) Do you not see that He is giving us all the license to penetrate the heavens, for this is our nature? What does Islam do? It brings human beings to their natural position: that you are unrestricted. "Go forth, have no restraints in yourself. Go forth; achieve whatever there is to be achieved. Delve into the depths of the oceans and reveal the secrets of the ocean. Go into space and find out what mysteries lie there, conquer it all, inhabit it all, it's all for you. You are an unending species I have created." And what does God do? He takes utmost pride at this search, at this growth, this evolution. Are you going to tell me that a teacher wants his students to be uneducated? Does any teacher take pride in uneducated students? Or does the teacher take utmost pride when his students begin to challenge him, pushing knowledge further? Are you telling me that a father takes pride in a son always being at the mercy of the father's decision and not being able to take his own decisions? Or does the father take pride when the son and the daughter come of age, and say to the father, "Now sit back and we will take over the business empire"? God has instilled that nature in the father and in the instructor. God by priority has the same nature. He takes pride in Adam and says to the angels, "Despite the bloodshed and corruption, even then I take pride in him, now prostrate to him." Imagine what we must have despite the bloodshed and corruption that Allah takes pride in Adam and gives him the knowledge of all the Names. What will this knowledge do inside? It has to bubble up and come out. Adam has all this inside him. We are the spectacles of Adam, we are the reflections of Adam – this has to manifest itself. So, what does Islam do? It brings human beings to that level of their nature which is to be unrestricted, and that is what the Quran says:

> *Those who shall follow the [last] Apostle, the unlettered Prophet, whom they shall find described in the Torah that is with them, and [later on] in the Gospel: [the Prophet] who will enjoin upon them the doing of what is right and forbid them the doing of what is wrong, and make lawful to them the good things of life and forbid them the bad things, and lift from them their burdens and the shackles that were upon them [aforetime]. Those, therefore, who shall believe in him, and honour him, and succour him, and follow the light that has been bestowed from on high thought him – it is they that shall attain to a happy state.* (7: 157)

The Prophet broke the shackles that were tying the people down. He lifted the weight that was pinning them to the Earth and turned a nomadic, warring tribe into a league of nations. He turned people that were illiterate into refined moral human beings and the greatest poets; from people who did not know more than the shimmering sands of Arabia to explorers; from people who were insecure and worshipped stones, to the people who are inventors and fathers of the scientific revolution that took place during the so-called golden period of Islam. What does Islam do? It brings people to that nature in which they are totally unrestricted.

What does this paradigm of unrestricted and unfettered growth mean? It says wholesomely submit to Allah; Allah has no limitation. Seek as much knowledge as you can; Allah is absolute in being the moral agent. Become a righteous moral agent, display angelic gems within your own character. Allah is the absolute focus, arrive at the pedestal of spirituality that you yourself begin to mirror ʿĪsā the son of Maryam – *that* is "God-centricity." This process of putting away, throwing aside and breaking all boundaries is known as the process of "liberation". So, "Islam, God-centricity, and Human Liberation" is the title of these talks. Wholesome submission to Allah – Allah, the principle of absolute completion. The process of liberation is the process of *lā ilāha*: there is no boundary, go forth and claim your glory. Now, before we conclude, think about this: If we were to define Allah as the giver of life, and we do not understand the meaning of "the giver of life," what will happen? It will curtail us. Muslims, as physicians, will never study the area of medicine that entails reviving dead bodies because theologically in their minds there is a boundary: "God gives life." On the other hand, suppose through modern advancements we are able to resurrect dead people. What will it do? It will shatter the very basis of our faith. This is what limited notions do to us: *they restrict our growth*. Just like the Christians who stated that the supremacy of human beings is based on the centrality of our being at the centre of the universe. As soon as the premise is broken, the rest of the theology built upon it is shattered – and Christianity as a result loses credibility to a great extent. But Allah explains so gloriously within the Quran that ʿĪsā resurrected the dead through My command, through My permission. Can you not see how Allah leaves these windows open? What a phenomenal book the Quran is. I am not saying that Allah does not give life: Allah gives life, Allah creates, Allah feeds. When one says, "O Allah, feed the poor," it is the human hand through which God provides sustenance. How beautiful is the hadith in which Allah says that on the day of reckoning, "I will surely tell you, 'I was hungry you did not feed me. I was naked you did not clothe me.'" How beautiful is this hadith. So when we clothe the naked, it is Allah clothing because Allah inspires us to clothe the naked. It is Allah sending that garment through us as agents to the one who is supplicating. When we say, "O Allah cure us!" what happens? Somebody makes a breakthrough in medicine that cures us. Do we say, "O man, you cured me"? No, we say, "O Allah, you are the one who has cured me *through* him." Allah is the giver of life. He can give it through ʿĪsā, or he can give it without ʿĪsā. Allah is the creator: He can create the Himalayas though a volcanic explosion, and he can create the Eiffel Tower through me and you. We need to understand things in a much broader way.

Ḥusayn ibn ʿAlī, how liberated the man is. I will give an example: if we are in a plane and it takes a nosedive, we would be filled with panic. What this reveals to us is our real state, the real me. The real me is not the one who sits so calm and composed in front of you; the real me is the one to be seen at the time of panic, at the time of crisis, at the time of test. Imagine if at that point there is a person who can overcome this panic, who has acquired their soul through Godliness. They can reason within themselves and say, "Well if this plane is going to crash then I will die. My time in burning my blood like this isn't going to make a difference. So I might as well sit calmly, because there is also a possibility that the plane may not crash in which case I don't want to die of a heart attack anyway." Imagine if a person could logically think through this situation. Imagine if a person can go beyond that and say, "Actually, O Lord, I embrace my destiny. As you can kill me through the crashing of this plane, you can kill me in my seat when I am not panicked by the fear of death. You can take me in any way, however you please." Imagine now if there is a person who grows through this threat and comforts the others and says, "This is not the end, this is the beginning of a beautiful world."

As Ḥusayn was being attacked and the outer circle of his army became fearful of death, they looked at Ḥusayn and said, "Look at Ḥusayn, ʿAbbās and Akbar, their faces are fearless; but look at the smile on the face of Ḥusayn. Look at the serenity and contentment." When Ḥusayn heard this, he smiled at them and said, "My grandfather has said, 'Death is a bridge from this world to the eternal gardens and to Allah.' Why should we fear death? Why should we not embrace it?" When he said this, the impact that it had upon all was such that a person was at the Kaʿba clinging to its cloth asking Allah to forgive him for killing Ḥusayn and his people. They said to him, "Do you have no shame? You outnumbered them and you killed them so brutally." He said, "By Allah, we killed them to save ourselves. They were running to death. They were running to death as a baby turns to the bosom of its mother. The only way we could save ourselves was to kill them." This is how it impacted them. Now imagine if a person can sit back and console others and increase their spirituality. *This is Ḥusayn*. He has conquered his fear and his anxiety. You do know that fear is manmade; danger is real. What Ḥusayn displays is something we cannot imagine.

Night Two

Yesterday we stated that the whole of this world is in a state of motion – a dynamic, incessant motion toward the completion of its own potential that is within it. It does not allow for any stagnation or any pauses. It is constantly bursting forth. It is constantly showing itself, elaborating itself and completing its own journey. In this process it cannot be restrained. Every form of restraint results in a violent event. If we look at the stars, when they devastate and deplete their energy, they explode creating newer galaxies and producing newer stars. It is always a growth process. If we were to look at the ratio of life to the ratio of death, life outnumbers death. Humanity has been evolving despite the challenges it has faced. Everything in this world is growing and whenever it is restrained it results in a violent event, and that violent event is there to promote further growth. The world, as she matures, results in volcanoes, Earthquakes, and what we call "natural evils," but they are there to promote further growth, further elaboration and further maturity. Similar is the state of human beings.

The human being is always on the move, always growing. This is the fundamental condition of the human being whether it is a physical one, procreating, advancing; or whether it is an intellectual one in which it wants to grow and elaborate. This is the fundamental nature of everything around us, ourselves included. But for us, beyond the physical surge of elaboration, growth, evolution and realization of that potential that is within us, there is also an intellectual facet in which we need to make sense of things around us. There is this yearning, a thirst within us to know, to conquer, to overcome obstacles. Strange is the story of human beings; we thrive under challenge. As soon as an obstacle is placed in front of us, we want to overcome it. As soon as a limitation is given to us we want to break it. We know no limitations, we know no boundaries, there is no stopping us. This is our fundamental nature.

We need to make sense of our world at large, but when we make sense of our world it not only restrains our growth, but it brings us into a state of confusion. On the one hand, we need to understand the world in order to make sense of it, in order to place things into their proper categories. But whatever sense we make of the world, ultimately and inevitably it is restricted because our worldviews are confined within a set of parameters; and anything that is within parameters cannot sustain the curiosity of that which has no parameters. If we are always in a state of unending motion, then any worldview that we set up for ourselves will inevitably be restrictive. To break through these boundaries requires great courage, but whether human beings display that courage or not, inevitably they will break through those boundaries for there is no stopping this motion. This results in violent events, in revolutions, in change of power and authority; from feudalism, to capitalism, to presumed communism. We are *always moving*.

Worldviews are always accommodating growth to a certain extent, and beyond that they restrain. In fact, as Hegel described, our process is dialectic. How is it dialectic? We form a worldview; this is a thesis. But in formulating the thesis we are also setting up parameters in which we will operate. Then the evidence contrary to it mounts, and we perform a process of tearing it apart; this is the antithesis. Then, together with the thesis and antithesis, we synthesize and form a broader worldview, and from that point forward it's a constant motion of elaboration, restriction, challenging and further elaboration. In fact, the prophets have done this very thing. They have displayed this very thing within the Prophetic trend. If you look at the successive prophets that have come, they have always challenged the human mind. They have always broadened their worldview; they have always given human beings a greater paradigm in which to exist so that they may flow towards their completion. This is the very nature that we see in the renewal of the Sharīʿah one after the other. In essence the Sharīʿah of Mūsā and ʿĪsā is no different from that of Ibrāhīm, and that is why they are called the Abrahamic faiths. Likewise the essence of the Sharīʿah of the Prophet of Islam is no different from that of Ibrāhīm or Mūsā or ʿĪsā. What has changed? The change is to accommodate further growth. What was happening at every level was that the prophets were giving something quite magnificent, beautiful and essential. They were providing a framework for unlimited growth, but because they had to formulate rules and regulations, morals and values, for those people in their context, the people, because of their naivety, took those formulations as ends within themselves. Hence there was a need for a new prophet to review the faith and return it to its original essence of flexibility, the essence that allows for unlimited growth. Hence, we see a succession of prophets who came and looked at the goodness of what the previous prophet had left and supplied it with their own forms. This was the process of thesis, antithesis and synthesis. It flows on the basis of "there is no god, but God". *Lā ilāha* is the breaking of the former paradigm; *illa Llāh* is the creation of a newer one. But here, the *illa Llāh* eventually becomes restrictive, *it* becomes the *lā ilāha* because feeble human minds have projected them onto the teachings of the prophet without understanding the essence of what the prophet was trying to convey. So a newer prophet comes, unravels it and brings it back to the essence and reformulates it.

The renewal of the message by each prophet is a constant process that is supposed to occur for all times and places. In fact, the best and most befitting paradigm ought to be based on "no finality". The human mind should mature now to a level where it can never be challenged anymore. The previous human mind, as soon as the

Earth was understood not to be the centre of the universe, was challenged. As soon as somebody resurrects the dead, the religious theological mind will be challenged. Today, if an alien were to descend upon the Earth, it ought to be something that we expect and accept; it should not challenge us at all. We ought to just say, "Yes, this is an event that was possible, and it has occurred, so what is the big deal?" To have a paradigm of "no finality" is to have a system in which everything and anything is possible.

Therefore we have to construct a worldview within a broader framework of no finality so that whenever it is challenged, we can revise it with ease without the need of complexities, confusions, bloodshed and revolutions. If we can arrive at that point of creating a paradigm that allows for unlimited growth and can be revised constantly by itself, then we have achieved it – and this is what God-centricity does, and Islam is supposed to do. If we look at Islam, it is wholesome submission to Allah, Who by definition is the most unlimited absolute principle of perfection. Allah is unlimited, you and I are the breaths of the Merciful. As He states in the Quran, "And when I have formed him fully and breathed into him of My spirit, fall down before him in prostration!" (15:29).

If our focus is God, and God is the unlimited and the perfect, then potentially we too are unlimited and perfect. The potential vested within us yearns to show and actualise itself, and the most befitting paradigm therefore is the one that liberates us through no finality. This is what theology is supposed to do for us. Belief in God is supposed to be a point of liberation, not a point of constraint. God can never be God if he does not allow for new challenges after creating us as inquisitive and challenging beings. If we did not challenge the status quo, how would we fulfil the purpose that God has placed within us? If we were to accept each and everything at just face value, how would we ever evolve? The fact that we struggle, the fact that the faiths come to a stage where they find an internal strife within them and they say, "Our belief system does not accord with life at hand and the dictates of life." The dictates of life are broader than the dictates of faith. What they misunderstand is that faith never dictates restrictions; it is the feeble minds of the faithful that construct the restrictions around the unlimited essence of faith. This challenge is what is encouraged by the process of Islam liberating us at all points. God is that principle that allows us to become complete. We yearn Him and He yearns us. The fact that His spirit is within us shows that we cannot be stopped.

Before we go into today's topic, consider this: that the Popes within Christianity were able to issue statements and mobilize the Christians into the Crusades that took place. They were able to do this a thousand years ago. Today's secular state, where Mr. Tony Blair proposed waging of war against Iraq on the basis of Saddam possessing weapons of mass destruction, is the same secular state that took to the streets in protest for the human rights of the other, the Iraqis. Imagine this, Christianity, with its proclamation of love and mercy, kindness and forgiveness for the other, was able to mobilize people into killing other people in the name of God, and yet here in the secular state people who are not supposed to be Godly, who are not supposed to be religious, are displaying Godliness and religious morals in standing for the rights of the other who is seen as the adversary and the enemy. On the grounds of humanity, the people challenge their own state.

Ask yourselves a simple question, which sort of world do you and I look forward to? Clearly, we are all seeking a world that is one of goodness. If you and I did not have any hope for a good world, would we be sitting here so hopeful of expanding our business empire tomorrow? Would we be educating our children? Would we be creating such beautiful halls and buildings? Would we be thinking of expanding? Whether we like it or not, our inbuilt nature is one of expansion, one of growth, one of positivity. Even though the religion we have inherited dictates that the world of tomorrow is a bleak world, a world of darkness, loss of morality, loss of spirituality, an unworthy world, this world that is in our heads is the world that stops us and stagnates us. But the real light of God that is within us, the real Islam within us, it wants expansion, goodness, harmonious coexistence and hence, we have this community participating in interfaith dialogues. As opposed to condemning every faith to the pits of hell and banishing the whole world to a pitiful end, the community in itself demonstrates an inner truth that is not demonstrated in its own worldview informed by its religion. The community wants to go forward. It has interfaith dialogues. It looks forward to a glorious tomorrow in which it wants harmonious coexistence. It is a community which stands for human rights regardless of religion, colour, race, or what have you. People in this community are participating in politics for a better tomorrow not only for itself but also for everyone else. At a level of worldview, most communities that are religious, at the level of their outlook, feel that everybody is condemned and the world is a pitiful place. But at the level of their actions they are displaying something else. They are displaying a positive attitude – a want for expansion and growth. This is inner Godliness that is calling them. This results in a conflict between (1) an intellectual worldview that has been constructed and influenced over many centuries by human thinkers like Aristotle, Newton, Einstein, or by religion and (2) the inner reality. This is where the struggle comes from.

The most befitting paradigm is of "no finality," in which whatever worldview we construct can be examined and re-examined. If it restricts and bars human growth it should not result in a state of confusion, bewilderment and fear. In fact, it should result in a state of confidence to challenge it and to go forward. Allah, if He has vested me with this potential, then I have enough confidence in my Lord Who has breathed His spirit into me that He will honour me. If truly I am surrendered to my Allah then by Allah I am not afraid. Then I say "O Allah, this is Your creature, speaking with the truth that You have placed inside me. What I have understood from what I have been taught and from what You are dictating from within my nature are two different things. O Lord, You have given me this life as a single opportunity – I will not let it go to waste. I will ask those pertinent questions until I get the answers. But Lord, if I were to know that this is what You want then I would prefer what You want above what I want. O God, I will not rest until I am true to what You have vested within me." So, the most befitting way in which we should understand the world, is a world with no finality.

I am going to give these examples as we advance in the talks. It was a popular belief in our communities that Imam Ḥusayn had seventy-two companions. The way in which the community thought was that the camp of Ḥusayn was made up of only seventy-two people. As soon as some scholars came forward and challenged this preconception of ours by arguing that there are reports that the Imam had one hundred and fifty companions, the whole basis of Ḥusayn's lofty stature shattered in their heads. But tell me, what difference should this make, whether he had seventy-two companions or one hundred and fifty companions? Ḥusayn is Ḥusayn. Then an Indian scholar by the name Mawlāna ʿAlī Naqan narrated in his book that Ḥusayn ibn ʿAlī ran out of water on the night of Ashura, so ʿAbbās with Habib and Akbar went and retrieved some water. The man was condemned to hell; the community was up in arms. "How dare you say Imam Ḥusayn was not thirsty for three days!" I will say here, are we to measure the sacrifice and worth of Ḥusayn by the number of days he was thirsty? Is that all the Imam is, a thirsty man!? What is going on in our communities that our way of thinking is so shallow and feeble that no sooner do we get new information than our understanding of this great man is totally shattered? It results in a mighty event, a revolution, a bloodbath, condemnation, apostasy, banning people, talking against each other? By Allah! I shall stand in front of Allah and in front of Muḥammad *rasūl Allah* and shall have to account for myself and everything I have done. My Ḥusayn will be in front of me on the day of *qiyāmah* and I shall have to look at this man in the face and he will say to me, "O Arif, you measured me in a sip of water and that is all I meant to you? What about everything else about me?" By Allah, even if Ḥusayn had been sipping water when the blade arrived at his throat he would still be the same great Ḥusayn ibn ʿAlī; and if Ḥusayn had lost water ten days prior to his *shahāda* he would still be the same Ḥusayn ibn ʿAlī. Ḥusayn is beyond seventy-two companions and beyond water. We have failed to understand this man for no other reason apart from the fact that we are not operating on the basis of no finality but have fixed views. If we adhere to the principle of no finality then imagine how open this world becomes. Imagine how we become receptive to the truth as the truth begins to flow into our chests. When people say, "God does not guide," it is not true; God always guides. It is me who is fixed in his views who does not allow for His guidance.

It is true, they say, that when the Twelfth Imam reappears the people will say, "This is not the right Islam. Go away, we know better than you." This is how much we are affected by the way we think. Our thinking shapes us and through our preconceptions we become biased. Every time the truth reveals itself to us in a new form we are tested: are we going to accept this truth or are we going to reject it? The Quran says one thing, but because my worldview is so narrow I will read something else into it. To give you a small example: suppose I have something against someone and I am carrying this prejudice against him forever in my mind. Then one day this poor fellow meets me and smiles at me, and what I think is, "See, he is plotting against me." When I harbour such thought, it's not a surprise that I don't think to myself that he is smiling at me because Allah has filled his chest with an angelic soul and he cannot help but smile. I can't appreciate this sentiment because of the state my mind is in. But if I could liberate myself then I would see his goodness as goodness itself. Therefore, in our opinion, the principle of no finality is the most apt. It is a worldview which opens our minds to new information. I am open enough in the state of Islam and surrender to accept it, to take it on board, to see what it means, to examine it, to see the truth therein. God-willing we will discuss how the Quran deals with this whole issue of liberating people.

This level of flexibility, of no finality, of being able to accept by fully letting go, is exactly what is meant by the terms Islam, God-centricity and human liberation. "Islam" means wholesome surrender; "God-centricity" means surrender to whatever is dictated by God because God is the most unlimited; "human liberation" means that I am the principle of lack and restraint, that I am the one who is restricted in my mind and my spirit and my morals, and that God is the ultimate principle of completion and absoluteness. If I were to yearn for Him through surrender then the only process that would come about is the one in which I lose my restrictions and begin to arrive at my own beautiful completion. That is the only process that conforms to our nature and this is the process I term as "no finality." We need worldviews, but we need to be clear that they are not sacred; they are not divine. They are human constructs based on religious or non-religious teachings.

The Quran gives a name to this utmost completion. It talks of it as *qiyāmah* whereby everything, be it me and you or the grand cosmos, is swiftly advancing towards its own completion. In terms of human completion, Allah refers to it as "salvation" (*falāḥ*) and says that to achieve salvation we are required to have (1) belief (*īmān*) in Him and in the Hereafter and (2) perform righteous deeds. There are two things that Allah demands from us insofar as creating a beneficial outlook is concerned. The first is to surrender to Allah; the second is to constantly strive and want to complete ourselves. The stage of completion that results is termed by Him as "salvation" and "success." Let us talk about salvation and success since we are a faithful community. We are here in order to find salvation and success. We devote ourselves to Allah in order to be successful on the day of *qiyāmah*. We want to go to Paradise as opposed to going anywhere else. We want to be people whom Allah is pleased with as opposed to those He is displeased with.

Now, if that is the case then we need to understand what salvation is. People of religion merely understand salvation to mean a belief system that informs their attitudes and their actions, and no more than that. Our understanding of what salvation means is straight forward. All I have do in order to be saved is say, "There is no god but Allah and Muḥammad is the Messenger of Allah," perform the prayer (*ṣalāh*) and fast as Allah has commanded me to, then I will be "saved." I am not saying that will be not be the case but I want to work into the issue more thoroughly. A Christian believes in the same way. A Jew believes in the same way. A Buddhist believes in the same way and a Hindu believes in the same way. There is no difference amongst any of them in this particular regard. Allah points this out in the Quran when He states that He has created for each community its own path (*mansak*) and for every one of them they have a direction. They are all the same but in their own way. I am not saying every religion is the same, but the Quran says the trend is the same for everyone. It is as if it is a human condition, a human need. But the Quran says, "Do you presume that by saying "I believe" that you will enter paradise and that I will not test you thoroughly." (29:2) When the Prophet performed his final ʿumra before the farewell Hajj, he stood on the mount of Marwa and summoned the people and said to them, "If you are from Quraysh but you are not righteous and do not mend your ways with Allah, I cannot do anything for you. Even if you say you believe in me, I will not be able to do anything for you. But if a slave should come to me without nobility in your sight because he is not from the tribe of Quraysh, yet he was righteous, he will have everything on the day of *qiyāmah* and I might be able to do something for him." Imam Ṣādiq states that "None of us have any kinship with Allah; we cannot influence a decision of God. If you are righteous and if you mend your ways with God, then we can do something for you. Allah will be pleased with you." All of these statements are saying that this salvation (*falāḥ*) is something other than what we have naively understood it to be. It is not a mere proclamation, "I believe in Jesus," and that's enough, I will go to Paradise.

I am giving you a scenario to think about very carefully. Allah says twice in Sūrah al-Nisāʾ (Chapter of Women) that "Allah will not forgive shirk; but other than shirk, He can forgive anything for anyone He likes." (4:48; 4:116) I am going to ask you a question;

it will be a shocking one. Saddam did not associate any partners with Allah – he did not do *shirk* – but he murdered people. He never bowed or worshipped an idol, nor did he ever proclaim Trinitarian beliefs by calling ʿĪsā "the son of God." Therefore, Saddam falls within the scope of that verse, and Allah can forgive whoever he wishes for anything they have done but He will not tolerate *shirk*. Can anyone's mind accept that? What does this mean? What is salvation? Allah does not need to punish such people. He says they create their own hell and they burn in their own inferno. Allah says: "be conscious of the fire whose fuel is human beings and stones which awaits all who deny the truth!" (2:24). Man is the fuel; man burns himself. Allah does not burn anybody. Allah makes it very clear in the Quran that you are the inferno in yourself. I pray, "O Lord, Extinguish the fire!" and Allah says, "I do so many times and you rekindle it." So forgiveness has a very different meaning – Yazīd, Shimar, Saddam, Khawli and every other oppressive person will face the consequences of their own evil actions, but still these are points to ponder over.

In any case, let us try to understand the meaning of success (*falāḥ*). What is success? Success is not a mere proclamation of any name or any faith. Yazīd did that, Saddam did that, Khawli did that, Shimr did that, and they killed the best of people. So, what is success within the paradigm of God-centricity, Islam and human liberation? Success is for anything to arrive at its fullest potential. So success for the seed of an apple tree would be to *become* an apple tree. Success for a fertilized ovum would be to *become* a foetus and a baby. Success for a student would be to learn, educate and actualise that education in the mind, not just to read and keep books and not understand anything of them. What is success for a human being? To arrive at the fullest glory vested within humanity. For a human being to *become* a moral agent who is worthy of being praised by Allah; to stand at such angelic pedestals of such glory that Allah takes pride in him; to achieve the fullness of intellectual curiosity and conquer the whole of the universe; success for a human being is to bring about a society with harmonious coexistence.

That is success for a human being – not only I as an individual, but society and humanity at large. For me today as a Muslim my concern is for my community, but when Prophet Muḥammad came there was no Muslim on the face of this Earth. He came for humanity at large. Bring me one prophet whose message is curtailed to a group. They have always wanted reformation for humanity at large, for humanity to move along the evolutionary track once again. Whenever they were stagnated intellectually, spiritually, morally, the prophets came to spur them on. My success is not success of just me, an individual, but success of humanity at large. This is the meaning of *falāḥ*. If a seed remains a seed that is not success. It has to tear itself apart to allow the tree to grow. The human mind has to be challenged for it to break through the boundaries that restrain it. Human morals have to become selfless morals for the sake of humanity, and beyond that for the human being to become God-like and acquire spiritual morality. This is what we mean by "success" of humanity and this is what we mean by utmost liberation through God-centricity in a state of surrender to Allah. Talking of a state of surrender, here is an example: when Gabriel visited Ibrāhīm at his ripe old age and said to him, "Ibrāhīm, Allah seeks to choose a friend upon this Earth," Ibrāhīm says, "Gabriel, lead me to the friend of God so that I may serve him." Gabriel says, "It is because of this, Allah has chosen *you*." Because of the state of surrender and fluidity within Ibrāhīm that Ibrāhīm submits and accepts that "whomever my God chooses, I will adhere to that. I will not let my bias come in the way."

Look at the first Muslims; they had worldviews when the Prophet came. The community of Medina could challenge itself to what he was saying to them, and as a result he liberated them and they went forward until eventually they arrived at the fullness of their existence; that was success. Every prophet has actively proselytized the message of Islam. Apart from Khiḍr and Yaḥyā who spent their lives in solitude, each prophet was a social reformer. They have challenged minds so that by doing so they could prompt growth within humanity, because they knew that the success of an individual lies in the success of the whole of humanity. Our story is a strange one. Our destiny is contingent upon each other. All of us are maturing; and success means that humanity has to come to the fullest actualisation of the potential vested in them through God-centricity. There is a beautiful narration that aptly explains the above eschatology. When Imam Mahdī appears he will not come to make you pray, because you will have been mature enough already to pray by that time. He will not come to make you pay the poor taxes, because you will already be paying it. He will not come to make you fast and do Hajj, because you will already know the value of these devotions and you will already be doing them. So what will he do? As the hadith says, "He will stretch out his merciful hand and place it upon your heads and drive your intellects towards their completion." This is the ultimate eschatology: the completion of the human intellect as a *collective* intellect. Therefore, success does not mean just a belief system in our mind that causes bias, but rather success is a substantive *process of growth* whereby human beings who are curtailed within the cradle of culture and community practices are able to break free and arrive at the fullness of the truth, emulate it, embrace it and share it with others so that they too may do the same. That is success. A seed has to embrace its destiny and grow into a tree that bears fruits to reach its success. A human being has to break free of his restraints to reach his completion. And this is what is signified by *qiyāmah*.

The process of liberation is supposed to take us to the yearning of utmost perfection and result in that completion that all of us want. This utmost liberation and completion can be seen in Imam Ḥusayn. On route to Karbala he sees a half-burnt tent. He approaches the tent and sees that there is an old woman in there who is a Christian, but because he is completely liberated he approaches her and sees to her needs. He is that liberated that not only does he speak to her with utmost dignity, but he even says to her, "I need the assistance of your son when he returns. Hasten him to me." In other words, he is asking for assistance *from a Christian* without any concern for which faith they adhere to. This is the level of his liberation; that he asks for help not from someone who he identifies as a Christian but from someone who he identifies as another human being. When we see this man's spiritual state of completion properly we realise that only he can be truly termed as the "ark of salvation". If we follow him properly, he will bring us to such a level of completion that humanity will take pride in us.

Night Three

We've stated that the whole process of Islam, God-centricity and human liberation is geared towards bringing the individual and the community alike towards their completion. The Quran calls this process salvation (*falāḥ*). *Qiyāmah* marks the utmost stage of completion. When we delve deeper into the workings of this and examine the book of Allah, we find that the completion of the self can only occur when restrictions are removed. Our completion is actually from within the self; the potential is already there; it does not come from outside — it comes from within. If it comes from within, then it is no longer the case that we must receive our completion from something outside, but rather that we receive it by removing the obstacles within the self to allow for its completion. Therefore, we have to go within and identify these obstacles in order to remove them so that we might grow. We gave examples of this: that a seed needs proper physical conditions for it to sprout and become a tree. From the Big Bang until now, the universe has been displaying itself in accordance with its own potential – it is elaborating; the only thing it needs to do is to remove its own obstacles that bar it from growth. Submission to Allah, or surrender to Allah, is the process of removing obstacles and self-imposed restrictions; there are no restrictions but we ourselves.

Surrender to Allah, then, is for us to yearn whatever beauty Allah has placed in us to manifest itself from within ourselves by letting go of our own restrictions. There are two different views that explain this, and both of them are accurate in their own context. The first is that we adorn ourselves with good human characteristics, and the second is that we actually free ourselves from bad characteristics. If we free ourselves from bad characteristics that are obstacles, the goodness will reveal itself properly. One is the understanding that we need to gain knowledge to complete ourselves, which is an accurate understanding. But more fundamental than that is that we should remove the obstacles within the mind in order for us to be able to embrace the goodness that is out there. For it stands to reason, no matter what we receive from outside ourselves, if there are blockages within ourselves then we will not interpret whatever we get from outside in an accurate way. Therefore, what we need to do is to let go of that which is within ourselves. This is what we mean by wholesome surrender to the most noble, absolute, complete, unrestricted principle which is Allah. This process of liberation begins from within the self.

Many people think that salvation and liberation are external to the human being, whereas in truth these are internal facets of a human being. A student will not become a qualified student by a pass mark if the student has not studied and actualised knowledge within his or herself. Possessing the biggest library in this world does not ensure success for a student until and unless they absorb the knowledge within those books and actualise them. The yardstick of success or failure is the student himself. It is from within, not from outside. Even if a student were to be given a pass mark, they would not be qualified to perform the task for which they have been given the pass mark. Salvation and completion, then, come from within. What bars them are the restrictions that are imposed by the self. The whole process of submission to Allah is the individual and the community removing their own restrictions through Allah, and through the removal of their own restrictions they automatically begin to complete themselves. As Rumi says, "O man who learns through rote, for you to retain your knowledge you would constantly need to read books. Why don't you do something else? Why don't you purify your inner self of its own restrictions? You will find that as opposed to inviting the springs of water to flow from outside into you, the real springs will gush forth from within you and flow outside." This is the difference. There is a real process that needs to take place. Whatever we have explained so far has been about letting go of our internal biases and restrictions through submission to Allah, Who is the loftiest principle of completion. What needs to be stated is that the whole story of Islam and salvation requires the individual and the community to become self-critical; to be able to let go of their own biases and restraints. These inner restrictions and obstacles are things Allah terms in His Book as *shirk*.

From the Quranic point of view, God-centricity means a full focus towards God in the sense that there is no association with God. Most people understand association with God as worshipping idols; this is not so. Worshipping an idol is not the point of *shirk*, it is an expression of *shirk*. The real *shirk* that Allah deems unforgiveable is something quite different. This is unforgiveable not because He does not want to forgive *shirk*, but because *shirk* is an unforgivable state. For example, an instructor says to the student, "I cannot pass a student who does not study, and who does not actualise knowledge." It is not that the teacher does not want to give a pass mark but rather that the student does not have the capacity of passing. The same set of circumstances apply to *shirk*: *shirk* is not something that God does not want to forgive; *shirk* is something that *cannot* be forgiven. *Shirk* in essence is actually the individual, not the Lāt and the ʿUzza or the Bhagwān and the stones. We can give association with Allah in a number of ways that all project the inner insecurities and state of conceited arrogance of the individual. When an individual is conceited and arrogant they become barred from growth. Tell me, what prevents me from listening to a contrary opinion? It is either my insecurity or my arrogance. In both cases I am barring myself from new information, and in both cases I will not grow. As a Western philosopher has said so beautifully and accurately, "Why do you fear contrary opinions? Think about it this way, if somebody were to come with a contrary opinion and you were to hear them out, if you find out that their opinion is wrong, it will be established for you that the position in which you stand and your opinion is most accurate. If you find that their opinion is more accurate than yours, then you have received your heritage: the truth. You have not lost anything; and if you find that that opinion is partially true then you have added to the truth you already have. Or you are able to cut away the falsities from the truth that you have. Why are you afraid? The reason you are afraid is either because you are insecure and you are barring yourself from growth, or that you are arrogant, in which case you are totally stagnant."

The Prophet of Islam said, "Throw dust on the face of the one who praises you." Why does he say that? Because as soon as somebody praises you, you become complacent about what you are. As soon as you become complacent it results in a loss of humility, barring the opportunity for further growth. That is why teachers deliberately do not overpraise their students, and parents do not go overboard in praising their children: so that the opportunity of growth cannot be lost. The reason why we do not accept the other is either because of arrogance or insecurity.

ʿAlī ibn Abi Ṭālib talks about Lāt and ʿUzza in Nahj al-Balāgha. He says, "Lāt and ʿUzza were not stones and sticks – these were statues that depicted corrupt, exploitive social orders and theologies, that were constructed by people, then projected onto stones and then worshipped. And those idols perpetuated those social exploitive orders that were chosen by people and then they were worshipped and made sacred." In other words, Lāt and ʿUzza are only stone and wood. They have nothing in them. Significance and meaning was given to them by the people who worshipped them. Lāt and ʿUzza were not the gods of the people; the people were the gods of Lāt and ʿUzza. In truth, they were not associating Lāt and ʿUzza with Allah. With introspection, when we analyse it, the true point of *shirk* is the very individual who worshipped Lāt and ʿUzza in his own image because he was the other god. A person who is a *mushrik* implicitly proclaims, "I am God." But then Allah says, "How can you evolve towards Me in surrender when you surrender to yourself. And even when you surrender to Me, you are surrendering to yourself in My name?" When we worship Allah today, most of us are worshipping only ourselves. Our insecurities are projected in the name "Allah," and then we worship Him. To give you an example, when the tsunami happened people pointed fingers at the existence of a merciful God. "If a merciful God exists why did He allow the tsunami to occur?" However, if this tsunami had come a thousand years ago, what would the people have said? "It was the show of the wrath of the Mighty God." And those who survived would have said, "O Lord, thank you for keeping us alive. You saved us," and they would have increased in their devotion to God through fear. A thousand years ago that tsunami would have been the greatest spectacle of the might of God. The same tsunami a thousand years on becomes a point of questioning the very existence of God. What has happened? Everything has been internal – we have worshipped God only in accordance with how we have set up God, whether we call Him Bhagwān, Lāt and ʿUzza or Allah, we are only worshiping the God that we have constructed in our minds. We are only worshipping ourselves. We are the greatest *mushriks*.

The blessed Prophet said, "If Abū Dharr was to know what is in the heart of Salmān about Allah, Abū Dharr would say, 'Salmān is a disbeliever (*kāfir*).' Abū Dharr is on the ninth level of faith (*imān*) and Salmān is on the tenth level of faith (*imān*). So if Abū Dharr was to know the God Salmān worships, Abū Dharr would kill Salmān." Therefore, *shirk* is not the stone and the rock. *Shirk* is me setting *myself* up as the other God, and this *shirk* has a lot of expressions. Those people were worshipping themselves through Lāt and ʿUzza. Similarly the Prophet has said that *shirk* is of two types: apparent (*jalī*) and hidden (*khafī*). *Shirk* which is apparent occurs when people bow in front of stones and rocks. But there is also a *shirk* which is hidden. The Prophet spoke about this type of *shirk* when he said, "*Shirk* will go unnoticed in the last of times just as an ant goes unnoticed in the darkness of the night as it crawls upon a black rock." The people asked, "What is this *shirk*, O Messenger?" He said, *shirk* is giving authority to other than Allah." An example of such *shirk* is when you wear a ring and without it you become insecure; that is a point of *shirk*. If you can discard this ring it shows you are truly a liberated soul, because the God that has put any potency in the ring is within you. "He is with you wherever you may be." (57:4) He has never left you.

Allah is insisting within the Quran that He can forgive anything for anyone, but not *shirk* because *shirk* is an unforgivable state. Islam therefore is the wholesome surrender to the utmost unlimited principle Allah, and this surrender has to be by the individual at the level of mind, body and soul totally. Unless this surrender comes at every level in the most wholesome sincere manner, Islam cannot work. Allah cannot begin to show Himself within the human being or the human community. The individual himself is the point of *shirk*. Now, let us take this idea further. Ninety-nine percent of the people end up proving the validity of the religion of their birth. Furthermore, they prove the exclusive truth of their persuasions to the extent that they can kill each other! This demonstrates that these people are not really thinking. They could have taken birth in any faith and been the same. The attitude of no finality and liberation from *shirk* can best be explained in the story that Rumi gives: there was an object placed inside a dark room. People went inside to examine it, each with a candle. One said, "It's a hose." The second one said, "It's a hand-fan." The third one said, "It's a pillar;" and the fourth one said, "It's a broom." Now these individual judgments were fine, but what happened subsequent to that is the one who deems it to be a hand-fan is ready to call the one who deems it to be a broom wrong, to the extent that they can kill each other. They are not ready to evolve and to share each other's knowledge. What happens is that the one who believes it to be a pillar cannot see beyond this. He is so arrogant that he gets stuck in this belief and therefore stagnates and kills for it, ruins himself and the other. Ninety-nine percent of people are doing this today.

Rumi said, "What if these people were to bring their candles and stand together?" They would get a bigger picture and realise that the pillar is actually a leg, the hand-fan is the ear, the broom is the tail, the hose is the trunk and this is in fact an elephant."

Therefore, if we were all to adhere to the principle of no finality we would see the reality of things. This wholesome submission requires that the individual does not become arrogant and conceited at any level of their existence, be it their emotional, intellectual or spiritual level. The person who worships Rām does so because Rām is truthful. He is courageous, knowledgeable, charitable, and most wise. The person who venerates Buddha does so because he is courageous, knowledgeable, charitable, and wise. The person who venerates ʿĪsā and Mūsā does so because they have the same qualities. The one who holds up the Prophet of Islam as the most magnificent example does so for the same reasons. You will find that every heart intuitively enjoys the *same* truth. They place different names on it and then fight over these different names, but are unable to accept and go beyond the names to see the truth for what it is. They themselves have restricted themselves: the truth is crying out from within them but their arrogance and insecurity does not allow them to evolve.

Therefore, in the process of Islam and liberation, God is the utmost principle of completion. What needs to go is the individual who is devoted to God (i.e. to eliminate the ego) before any liberation can take place and before the process of evolution can start. One needs to be able to say when faced with new information, "Let me think about it," instead of opposing and rejecting it outright because of the person who is saying it. When the blessed Prophet went to the Meccans they said, "He is a mad man, he is a poet, he is a liar!" The blessed Prophet would stand at the door of the Kaʿba and talk to the congregation. A small group of people would gather around him and a bigger group would gather around the smaller group. One person from the larger group would shout, "He's a mad man! "He's a liar!" Then another ten would join in, and soon enough the majority of the people would be shouting at the Prophet. This is called mob mentality. The Quran says in so many of its verses, "This man is not mad, he is not a soothsayer. Why don't you stand alone or in twos and think about the content of what he is saying? Does it make sense? If it makes sense then contemplate upon it, and accept it." This is what the process of Islam requires: that a person is able to fully let go.

As an Indian I truly salute our Hindu forefathers: they were the greatest Muslims. These people who were Hindus were open enough and ready to give a listening ear to Pirs of the Ismaili daʿwa who spoke to them. Those Hindu forefathers of ours were the truest Muslims because they submitted to Allah and took on knowledge for what it was worth, and they said, "The truth is our heritage and we will follow it where and as and how we find it." What happens today is that the same Allah that was in the name of Bhagwān, we have made him another Bhagwān. Every time human beings evolve, they end up constricting themselves at the individual level and the communal level. Today in the folds of Islam we do the same thing that the Pharaoh used to do. Pharaoh took his gold and silver with him inside his grave. Our mentality today is the Pharaonic mentality within Islam. Today we will pray a hundred unit prayer (*ṣalāh*) because we believe that a sack of one hundred units (*rakʿāts*) will come with us to our graves. But after praying those hundred *rakʿāts* we do not become more truthful, more sincere or less greedy. What have those hundred *rakʿāts* done to us? We think of God sitting on a throne with a book marking how many prayers we have performed for Him as if it was a tick box exercise. Of course not! Allah says, "You are sufficient for your own judgment on this day because you are the speaking Book, you have become whatever you have become and you are the final judgment onto yourself," (see Q75:13–15). Today we worship Allah in the same way that the pagans worshipped Lāt and ʿUzza.

Khawli, the killer of Ḥusayn ibn ʿAlī, was coming out of his house. His wife said, "Khawli, what do you intend?"

He said, "I am going to Karbala. Ḥusayn has come in rebellion against the Caliph of the time."

She said, "Ḥusayn is the grandson of the Prophet, the son of the daughter of the Prophet. How can you kill the most righteous? Ḥusayn is the Imam!"

Khawli said, "Whatever he may be, the Prophet has said whoever comes in revolt against the Caliph put them to death."

It was the inner belief within Khawli that he was projecting outside onto Islam. Otherwise he would immediately know that what he was saying makes no sense. This is exactly what is happening with all of us.

Islam, God-centricity and liberation means a state of fluidity within us in our submission to Allah at every point. Allah says, "Every day He manifests Himself in yet another wondrous glorious way." (55:29) We need to claim a newer glory within ourselves by arriving at a newer pedestal of inner liberation. The way Allah depicts *shirk* in the Quran is phenomenal. The Quran gives examples upon examples of *shirk*; it talks about a variety of different *shirks*. At one point Allah says, "That they say, we do not worship these things, save that they should take us closer to Allah." (39:3) As if Allah says, "How dare you say this! Did I authorise you to place these things as an intermediary between Me and you?" Allah says to the individual in the Quran, "Call unto Me, I am near." (2:186) Allah removes any intermediary between Him and His creature. His salient message is, "It is directly you and it is directly Me, everything else is a form of distraction."

The Meccans used to go into their houses through the back door when they would wear the robe for pilgrimage (*iḥrām*). Allah then says to them (I am paraphrasing), "There is no good in the practice of going into your houses from the back door. Goodness is to be God-conscious. Go through the front door. There is no value in these things; all these things you are doing in order to sanctify Me, they are becoming *shirk* in themselves, they are becoming distractions in themselves. Chop it all away. Get rid of them." The Prophet's teachings imply, "If you are truly God-centric then break all idols. Remove all the intermediaries between you and your God." You will not find a single verse in the Holy

Quran in this respect that gives importance to anyone but Allah and the individual.

When it comes to the story of salvation, read the Quran. Allah does not hold belief in any of the prophets as a central tenet for salvation. He says time and again, "Believe in Allah, the Hereafter, and becomes righteous and perform righteous deeds and you will get your salvation." Where has he placed any prophet in the story of salvation? As if He says, "Salvation is not proclaiming the names of ʿĪsā and Mūsā. Salvation is you becoming Godly and fulfilling your potential." That is salvation. Salvation is a seed becoming a tree. Allah says to the angels on the day of *qiyāmah*, "Did these people worship you?" And the angels would say, "Glory be to You, O Allah! They worship the Jinn." (34:41) The day on which Allah will summon all the prophets and say to them, "Do you know what happened on the Earth after you left?" They will say, "We don't know anything." (5:109) Allah says to ʿĪsā, "ʿĪsā, did you tell them to worship you and your mother other than Me?" ʿĪsā will reply, "Why would I say something of which I have no right. O Lord, I have no knowledge of what they did after I left. You know best. If You punish them, they are Your creatures. If You forgive them, You are most forgiving." (5:116) As if Allah says in the Quran, "Nothing comes between Me and My creature." He is constantly challenging the mind: that everything you are stipulating other than Allah is a form of distraction. This form of distraction has to be removed. In the story of human success, both intellectual and spiritual, Allah asks for the removal of everything that is between the individual and God. The Quran is adamant about this. It does not allow any practice that can come between Allah and the individual.

The salient principle of every religion has been this God-centricity, and the process of growth and evolution. The *sharīʿahs* that come have only been there to inform us of *how* this surrender is supposed to be. The essence has been the individual and God. God-centricity is thus like this: the individual is in lack, God is the principle of completion; "surrender to God" is an invitation to remove all the lacks one by one by one. In our religious communities we are taught not to question. But if a people do not question, how would they arrive at the truth? There are two types of things we can ask: "If it is proven that this is from Allah then I will believe that it is from Allah." But we dare not ask the subsequent question, "What does Allah mean by this?" Is this not our God-given right? In fact, Allah has placed this curiosity within us to ask and yearn for the truth. The basic point here is that going away from this state of liberating ourselves indicates a state of *shirk*. Whether as formalistic *mushrik* or formalistic Muslim, they are equally in a state of *shirk*. A person who is unable to grow is a person who has imposed self-limitations upon himself, and he is his own damnation. This is as true for a community as it is for an individual.

The Muslims are supposed to be the greatest, most righteous people favoured by God. If that is true, then why has no Muslim gone to the Moon by now? Why did the Muslims not split the atom or discover gravity or find a cure for cancer? Why are the Muslims so useless? There are almost two billion Muslims in the world, yet they are cursing the West. Can you truly curse capitalism when it is providing such a beautiful welfare system? Can we truly curse the political system in this country when it allows a Muslim to criticise the policies of its government with full amnesty? Can one find this in any Muslim country? Today, if you want to become the prime minister here, you can do so. Can one really condemn them? When the tsunami strikes the Muslim lands, the non-Muslims are the most charitable. Can we really condemn them? The biggest state of damnation and condemnation is that which Muslims have imposed upon themselves. And then they project this as something sacred and holy in the name of Allah, this Allah that we are worshipping also becomes a construct of our own imagination. It is nothing but that pagan mentality (*jāhiliyya*) that we have imposed on ourselves.

Islam, God-centricity, and human liberation asks for introspection, the removal of these self-imposed barriers, whether these barriers are the arrogance of the self or the insecurities created by the community. If the majority were right, then this example is befitting: there was a man on a stretcher being carried to his grave and there were about four hundred people in the funeral procession reciting, "There is no God but Allah" (*lā ilāha illa Llāh*). There was a man from another town looking at this funeral procession and he hears the person in the coffin screaming, "I'm alive, I'm alive, don't bury me!" So, this man says, "Look, this person is alive, can't you hear he is alive? Don't bury him." So a man responds, "Should I believe the four hundred that are saying he is dead, or should I believe the one who is saying he is alive?" The lesson here is that the majority is not necessarily true. Truth stands by itself. Truth proves its own self.

Islam, God-centricity and human liberation asks for the inner idol to be removed. This inner idol is our insecurity or arrogance. If you are arrogant then you are preferring yourself over Allah. If you believe that Imam Ḥusayn only had seventy-two people with him and you are not ready to believe anything else, then you have created your own god and are projecting this self-made god onto the name "Allah," making you the biggest *mushrik*. If, on the other hand, you are frightened into submitting to something that does not make sense simply because the majority is saying so, then this is your own insecurity. This was exactly the state of the Meccans. In the same vein, when ʿĪsā went to the Jews they found what he was saying very strange. They said, "How can he challenge the status quo that has been placed by Mūsā." When you look at Islam within the Quran, how has God termed Islam? Islam of God in the Quran is not fasting, prayers and Hajj. Islam of God within the Quran is Ibrāhīm, Isḥāq, the children of Yaʿqūb, Ismāʿīl, Mūsā. They are Muslims. They do not have the rituals we have, yet they are all Muslims. The Prophet Yaʿqūb said to his children, "Don't die, save in the state of Islam." Ibrāhīm says, "O Lord, make me into a Muslim." What is a Muslim? A Muslim is not one who prays or fasts or goes for Hajj; these are merely expressions of surrender to Allah. Islam in essence is to prefer Allah over the self. Islam is God-centricity, focus towards Allah, and the process of inner and outer liberation. This is the essence of Islam; everything else is a trimming of Islam. Wahab, the one who was martyred with Imam Ḥusayn, did not bow to Allah, nor did he perform Hajj; yet he achieved the loftiest status of salvation in a state of Islam and through the essence of Islam. Ḥurr never prayed behind Ḥusayn acknowledging him as the Imam; he was in the enemy camp. He came and joined the ranks on the morning of Ashura and obtains the loftiest rank. The real surrender, the real state of Islam, is that inner and outer giving of the self to Allah in its entirety. "O Lord, I am open to the truth as and how it may come. I am not stifled by my own arrogance. I am not perturbed by my own fears and insecurities. If the truth comes from the mouth of a non-Muslim, then that is Islam and I will accept it and evolve through it."

What do you find in the stories of the Prophets? The Prophets by and large left the majority of their community. Prophet Lūṭ and Prophet Ibrāhīm – they came out of their community, leaving the majority so that only a very few people arrived at the truth. But in the case of our Prophet, he distanced himself from the majority but then the majority flocked to him. The Prophet is the only one to whom the majority flocked, and therefore he was the most successful man on the face of the Earth. ʿAlī ibn Abī Ṭālib says, "Do not feel afraid because of the scarcity of the followers of truth, for the nature of the truth is such." There is a Prophetic hadith that says that there will be seventy-three sects in Islam, and out of the seventy-three, seventy-two sects are going to hell. Does this hadith make sense? Because the Prophet was asked, "What will you do for us on the day of Judgment?" he said, "Allah told me that I will allow you to give forgiveness to half of your Ummah. I did not accept that, so Allah gave me the option to individually intercede for each one of you, and I accepted that instead." How can the man that says he will intervene for us individually say that seventy-two sects of his Ummah are going to hell? We have to question and be wary of hadiths that instil bias and arrogance inside our hearts. How can this hadith be correct? When Allah is giving paradise to the qualifying Jews and Christians, can He really drive seventy-two sects of His Prophet's Ummah into hell? Any thinking mind would say that I cannot allow such hadith to instil this arrogance and this bias in my heart. Today this kind of hadith is what plagues our minds: that everybody else is going to hell. That whatever they are saying is wrong. This is totally inconsistent with the state of Islam, God-centricity and human liberation because God-centricity and liberation dictates that we *think*, that we read the words of God and submit to Him. Imam Ḥusayn explicates so beautifully the meaning of monotheism (*tawḥīd*). He so wonderfully understands Allah. In his supplication on the day of ʿArafa a year prior to his martyrdom he states, "O Allah, when were You hidden that I needed to see You? Blind are the eyes that do not observe You. O Allah, when were You far that I needed to gain proximity to You? You were always near, it was I who has remained at a distance from You. O Lord, what has he found the one who has lost You? And what has he lost the one who has found You? O Lord, should I look at the stars, the sun and the moon to guide me to You when I see You standing before it, above it and below it? Should Your handiwork be more manifest than You Yourself who creates what You create?" This is how proximate Ḥusayn is to Allah, removing every obstacle between himself and his Creator.

Night Four

We stated previously that Islam means a wholesome state of surrender; surrender at the level of the intellect, emotions and at the core level of our being that forms our personalities and attitudes. It means a state of fluidity and a state of non-stagnation, where the human being comes exactly in line with the property of the state of existence, which is one of elaboration, self-realisation, evolution, going from weakness to strength, from strength into greater strength, and the fulfilment of that beautiful potential that is vested within us. If we could wholesomely give ourselves to Allah with an attitude that there is no finality, then what is true today may not be true tomorrow, or it may lead into a greater truth. If the people following the Jewish faith could have understood this, they would not have resisted the teachings of ʿĪsā. If the Jews and Christians had upheld this state of no finality, the state of beautiful fluidity, they would not have rejected the message of the final Prophet. When people moved away from this fluidity into a state of rejection, they moved into a state that is unforgivable, because forgiveness means a state of growth, of removal of impediment; you cannot forgive a state of self-imposed impediments and restrictions. If I choose to be in a particular way, nothing can move me from that way. It is only I who can move from that restrictive state. Therefore, Islam and surrender to Allah, the ultimate principle, requires a state of fluidity from within.

Allah terms this sate of fluidity as the process of facing Allah and being monotheistic. Islam is described within the Quran as merely a state of wholesome surrender to Allah, and preferring Allah above and beyond the self and human society. Wherever the truth comes from, accept the truth. The people that fail to do this are called disbelievers (*kuffār*) in the Book of God.

In His Book, Allah says, "Indeed the statement of truth has been confirmed for the majority of them, and they will now not believe!" (36:7). Allah does not hesitate in the Quran to declare the formal Muslim as a *kāfir*. The root of the word is from *ka-fa-ra*, meaning to hide or to cover. The real *kāfir* is the one who hesitates from accepting the truth since they are hiding the truth. Now, you might ask, "This does not sound logical; they have not received the truth so how can they hide the truth?" Allah explains this as something quite different. He states that the truth is within you as your existential condition. You are a creature that finds no rest from within. You have no stagnation. You have no boundaries for you to restrain yourself from. Stagnation means you are performing *kufr* at the greatest level; and for you to become complacent in the position that you are shows that you are doing *shirk* – and this *shirk* will not be forgiven because you will not grow.

Allah says in the Quran, "I took a pledge from you, am I not your Lord? They stated, 'Yes, indeed, You are our Lord'." Allah says further in the Quran, "Lest on the day of *qiyāmah*, you turn to Me and you say to Me, 'O Lord, our forefathers did this and we merely followed them, why do you chastise us for a sin that they committed and we were conditioned in that sin?' Or that you come to Me on the day of *qiyāmah* and you say to Me, 'We had no knowledge of this'." (7:172) The knowledge is inbuilt within your system. You are hardwired to be fluid, to flow with the truth, to evolve and to grow. Any restriction therefore is self-imposed by you yourself. Allah says, "Say to the people of the Book, come together with us on the basis of the worship of one God and on the condition that some of us do not take others as Lords apart from Allah." (3:64) The Companions (*ṣaḥāba*) went to the Prophet and said, "O Messenger of

God, we understand the first part: that we shall not worship other than Allah; but the latter part of the verse that we will not take each other as Lord other than Allah, what does that mean?" The Prophet said, "That we will not listen to each other if they are conflicting with Allah." What does "conflicting with Allah" mean? Allah is the principle of ultimate completion; if there are any teachings from any mouth, be it from a person who is religious or priestly, the verse is saying and the Prophet is categorically saying, "We will not take our priests and our learned as mouthpieces of God or follow them in the name of God if they conflict with God."

Allah is insistent upon the removal of every barrier. The message He gives us in the Quran is that, "All these things are a distraction." Your mere focus ought to be towards Allah, God-centricity, a state of fluidity, and a state of evolution. Allah clarifies everything in a beautiful way when He states, "Those people that you call onto other than Allah, they do not hear you till the day of *qiyāmah*. And if they were to hear you, they cannot respond to you." (35:14) On the day of *qiyāmah* when the people who called out to others go to them, and they see that those they used to call upon absolve themselves of the people who used to call them, they will say, "If only we could have a second chance and we could absolve ourselves of all the people that we used to call." (2:167)

Allah is insistent in the Quran that in the state of fluidity you need to face Allah wholesomely without any restrictions, and your entire focus should be only towards Allah. Allah gives multiple examples in the Quran that anything other than Allah is a means of distraction, but more than that what Allah expresses in the Quran is that those you call upon and place values on never proclaimed such values because on the day of *qiyāmah* they will say, "O Lord! We had no knowledge of the *shirk* that they were doing." Our role models such as the Prophet and the Imams are perfect examples of individuals who expressed these truths. The Prophet of God, looking at the acute nature of idolatry within his community, where the people used to attach values to idols and drawings, stated: "Break the idols and do not draw anything least you be distracted." He stated further: "Leave the mosques unadorned. Let there be no distraction in the mosque so that your focus can be solely towards Allah." Let Allah become the central tenet. There should be a pure monotheistic message so that we arrive at this state of God-centricity and inner and outer fluidity towards Allah.

The way that the Imams expressed this focus towards Allah is quite phenomenal. In the supplication *Jawshan al-Kabīr* it says, "O the Physician for the one who has no physician, the Support for the one who has no support, the intimate Companion for the one that has no intimate companion." The monotheistic message expressed by the Imams can be understood in two ways: on the one hand, when a person is sick they go to every door, but after failing to receive any help they run to mosque and invoke Allah. But when there are qualified physicians who can provide a cure, even then the vision of the monotheist is such that they say, "Allah, it is only You who is doing this and nobody else." This is the monotheistic message the Quran is providing: that your focus is only Allah. The hand that cures you is not an independent hand, but one through which Allah provides His help. This is how Allah in the Quran removes all forms of *shirk* in order to liberate the human being.

You and I are a product of our societies, cultures and our religions. We are born with a preordained DNA. In addition, our culture and religion shape our worldview and how we understand and relate to the world. Cultures and religions condition us to such an extent that the once unrestricted being that came from the Merciful is immediately restricted intellectually. These intellectual restrictions bring with it spiritual and psychological restrictions that shape our attitudes and define our identities. When a person comes of age, that is not the "real" person as created by Allah. The real, unlimited, unrestricted beauty of God has been covered and fashioned. It has been moulded into something created by these external influences. In all of these individuals, whether they are born into the house of the Prophet or an Imam, or in the house of Pharaoh, they are all the same – all of them are being restricted in a different way. All of them take on the same journey. This is the story that Allah describes in the Quran.

Allah says (I am paraphrasing): "In the whole story of liberation, you need to be *objective*. You cannot accept any truth without question or just because it has been supplied to you by your forefathers or by religious authorities." Allah insists within the Quran that the basis of right and wrong must be a rational one. Reason is universal; it is based on an intuitive property. For example, why do we say truth is better than lying? It is because truth is productive. It encourages production, evolution and growth. Why does reason find truth productive? Because it is an existential property of growth. Reason is secondarily deriving these judgements from the core of existence. Existence is always flowing, evolving and elaborating. Reason, based on that property, will conclude that that which is productive is right. Based on this understanding, speaking the truth is not always right, giving life is not always better than taking life, because if giving life poses a threat (for example, if you are being attacked by your enemy), in order to save yourself you have to defend yourself and therefore kill your enemy.

According to a story by Saʿdī, one of the major Persian poets and literary men of the medieval period, there was a criminal brought in front of a king. The criminal pleaded, "Save me, spare me, I will devote myself to you," but the king said, "No, my judgement is final, put him to death." Saʿdī says, "And when the cat becomes hopeless of receiving any gifts from her master, she does not restrain herself but meows the loudest that it can." So, the man began to shout abuse and curses at the king. The king turned to his vizier and asked what this man was saying. The vizier explained that the man was eulogising the king for his sense of justice and righteousness. The king smiled and ordered the man to be freed. The other vizier said this was slander (*khiyāna*), that the man had been swearing at the king's mother and father. The king replied, "A lie through which good can come is better than a truth through which evils comes." The Quran is insistent on rational discernment. Do not look at what is being said or even who is saying it, and practice anything regardless of how long it has been practiced if it does not make sense.

The following example explains rational discernment very clearly. For example, in Uḥud there were a small number of people with the Prophet who were defending him when all others had fled. The only two people concurred upon by historians who were definitely with the Prophet were Imam ʿAlī and Ṭalḥa. Ṭalḥa was a champion of Islam. When the people saw Ṭalḥa and Zubayr on the opposite camp in the battle of Jamal, they went to ʿAlī ibn Ṭālib to ask how it was possible that Ṭalḥa and Zubayr, such grand companions (*ṣaḥāba*) of the Prophet and devotees to Islam, were on the wrong side? Imam ʿAlī advised them to look at the truth and *discern through the truth* and not look at the people to discern the truth. What this means is that truth stands alone: it proves its own self. Allah here is respecting the human being to the utmost, that your mind is no different than that of the Prophet in this respect.

Culture and religion supply us with the answers before we have even asked the questions. Before we can ask what is right and what is wrong, our society has already determined the answer for us. Before we can ask about the genders, we have already been taught that being a man is better than being a woman. This restricts the process that Allah initiates in the Quran – one of rationality and enquiry. Allah prompts this question throughout the Quran, "Do they not think? Do they not understand?" Allah states in the Quran, "Having hearts wherewith they understand not, and having eyes wherewith they see not, and having ears wherewith they hear not. These are as the cattle – nay, but they are worse! These are the neglectful." (7:179) Man, the crowning glory of God, how can he be so moved away from the natural state of existence? What curtails you is you yourself. The central message of the Quran is liberation of every human individual in their individual human capacity, and through that the liberation of the community as a whole. God-centricity is then emphasised by Allah, who commands us to scrutinise everything and see if it makes sense.

Night Five

Reason and rationality play a pivotal role in the whole process of liberation and God-centricity. This process of human life is for us to achieve the completion destined for us. We came to this world through our demand and our choice. We have to re-think our traditional theological position. It is not as we imagine it: that God knew all affairs prior to creating us, then He placed us here to act out His foreknowledge, and then He is going to punish or reward us on the Day of Judgment. Rationally that does not make any sense, and intuitively it does not sit well. If God knows everything prior to creation, then why does He put us on this Earth for us to act out everything that He already knows, and then punish or reward us? What I am saying is that at a rational level this concept does not make sense; and such a God is not worthy of worship. Such a God is inconsistent with our intuition, our existential position, our property of evolution and growth.

Think about this very carefully: if without my request, without my choice, God has originated me from non-existence and just said, "Be!" and I am – if it was truly like that, and He said, "Act out in this world," and He already knows what I am going to do – then that God would not be a merciful God. Which mother, knowing that her child will suffer, would deliberately allow her child to suffer? And after causing that child to suffer by creating the circumstances of their suffering, punish the child on top of that suffering? That does not make sense. Does this sort of a worldview make sense to anybody?

I often give this analogy, that the God we worship in the name of our religion and the sort of world we have constructed in our minds can be best depicted by this analogy: a person is inside a room which has a hundred doors, ninety-nine of which are booby trapped and lead to explosives that will destroy us. There is only one door that leads to another room – this is how a religious person understands life, that if by chance you can find that one door (because all other religions are wrong, only one is right), then we go into another room which has a thousand doors of which nine hundred and ninety-nine lead to damnation and only one leads to security. If Allah has placed such unending love, mercy, compassion and care in the heart of a mother for her children that she would sacrifice herself time and time again to secure the safety of her child, then how can a God who imparts a ray of His beauty to a mother that makes her so compassionate not be merciful? How can He lack compassion Himself? When we examine it rationally, we see that these things do not make sense. The Quran talks about us making a choice, making a demand to be in this world – a world of opportunity. God makes it very clear in the Quran, if only we read the Quran without our biases. Referring to the Quran, the Holy Prophet says, "This is light in darkness, guidance in misguidance. Whatever you want, take it from the Quran. Even if my hadith were to conflict with the Quran, throw them to the wall."

This Quran needs to be read. The questions in our minds need to be answered. But first and foremost, through reason we need to filter our belief system to see what makes sense and what is irrational. The sort of life that we live, the sort of world that we construct, is an irrational world. It does not make sense. We have all been faced with this question: "O Lord, is there nothing more to life than this?" That question prods at our hearts and minds. Is there no more to life than what I have understood? Yet we are so lazy, so insecure, so complacent in the sort of religions we have constructed, we will quickly reject the thought or we will quickly uphold whatever the religious speaker has said on a pulpit on a particular occasion to satisfy ourselves that we are in secure boundaries and can therefore sleep peacefully at night. We are delusional people. We delude ourselves. I often say this, that those people who think they are in the ark of safety, may God cause the effects of this "happy pill" to wear off and make them begin to see that they are in the deep ocean, drowning, and they need to vigorously use their hands and feet to swim to the shores of safety. How can anybody live in such a world? A world born of insecurity. A world born through lack of knowledge of God, through lack of courage, through lack of any foresight or any accuracy or any reason. This is the world of a religious person.

We stated that Islam is a whole process aimed at bringing us back in line with that existential property. The existential property is that we remove all obstructions, lack, restrictions, and evolve to the fullness of what awaits us. The process of Islam is like a seed in the journey that it takes. It needs to allow itself to be buried deep inside the ground, and then it needs to allow itself to break its chest, to be torn apart so that the plant can sprout from it. Until and unless these minds, these hearts, these attitudes do not give themselves to the sword of Islam, they can never emerge. They will only remain what they are. You may find grown people who have not grown at all since their childhood. In fact, the following anecdote shall explain this as we go into our subject.

Luqmān, the great sage, passed by a graveyard as he approached the village, and curiosity overtook him so he began to read the gravestones. They had tender young ages inscribed upon them – age of two, four, five, the maximum anybody had lived was ten. He goes into the village and enquires, "Was there a plague? What happened? Why were your children taken so suddenly?"

They said, "Luqmān, these were ripe old men of fifty, sixty, seventy, eighty and ninety."

He said, "Then why do not their gravestones bear witness to their ages?"

They responded, "Luqmān, we have only noted those of the years of their lives in which they lived as free-thinking men and women, for before that they had not even arrived into the world of the living."

***

We stated that Islam is a process that liberates us. The real Islam says make God your focus. Give yourself to God fully. Let Him nurture you. Let Him bring you to your completion. He is the Lord (*rabb*), the nurturer. He nurtures us in all facets of lack. He nurtures our physical being. Similarly, He nurtures our intellectual being, our emotional being and the spiritual facet that we have. In terms of the physical one we cannot restrain it: we are growing and nothing stops moving at the physical level until the moment it dies. At the level of the intellect, God says, "Think! Does any of it makes sense, is any of this reasonable? Can you actually accept such a thing?" He asks again and again and again. In the Quran He says, "O Jews, if you are saying this; O polytheists, if you are saying this; then know that God can never command something that is unjust and unrighteous." How can God say that God can never command something that is unjust and unrighteous? What is the yardstick by which the people can then accept the fact that God is speaking the truth? The yardstick through which the people can assent to this statement, that God is speaking the truth, is our reason and intuition; that if I were to believe in God then God would depict the peak of what I find as right in its glorious way. So, if I say speaking the truth is good, then God by priority would say speaking the truth is good. As if God says, "Through reason I will liberate you, but you need to give yourself to Me at that rational level."

Let us say something about how Allah modifies our attitudes through the use of reason. God, realising our state, asks for reason to be employed in the whole process of growth, liberation and evolution. We are born within the cradle of animality. In that cradle of animality we are imaginary individuals whose intellect has yet to emerge and begin to think. You see how with children we are able to frighten them: we say, "The Witch will come and consume you if you don't sleep. The monster will come upon you." The children are over imaginative. They fear the dark, they fear shadows, they fear sounds at night. These are irrational fears – we are born with this, and the process of liberation states that we need to go beyond these imaginary fears that we concoct. To explain this: danger is real; fear is manmade. We revert to that example once again: when the plane takes a nosedive, the danger is real – it could crash and we could die. Or there is a possibility that it might just pick up and we will live. But what happens at the point when the plane is dipping, when the engines fail? The danger is real, but our reaction of fear to that danger creates panic. The perspiration, the cries, the anxiety – none of these has anything to do with the fact of the matter. It's all being created by us. Reason is supposed to modify that. It is supposed to regulate us to come beyond these imaginary fears. If a person can reason at that point they will say, "Either the plane will crash and I will die, but if I cry and panic I might die of a heart attack anyway." If they could reason with the situation they would not panic.

You see, that child we thought was no longer, is still within us. There is a lot of insecurity. There is a lot of fear that we have yet not conquered. We have not evolved beyond that stage. If you want to see the real substance of a man, put him under a difficult situation and that is when you will see the real man for what he is worth. Allah says in Sūrah al-Nūr (Chapter of Light) about those who are bent on denying the truth and who are not growing, "Their state is like one who is at sea, the waters are stormy, waves are enormous, there is darkness, it is night, and clouds upon clouds, layers upon layers, so that if he were to take his hand out, he would not be able to see his hand." (24:40) Now Allah depicts the situation further, that such a person at that point will cry; he will lose all sense of surrounding of who is around him. He will cry out and implore, "O Lord, save me! And if You save me, I will never disobey You again." This is the real person that comes out. There is turmoil within us, but because we are on the shores of safety this turmoil is masked. It is a delusional world. For the person in the middle of the ocean who fears the wave overtaking him and killing him, when at the shores of safety that same person may have a blood clot travelling up his artery that will kill him even now. What difference is there between the two? What difference is there between the plane nosediving and me sitting here? I am in the same perilous position, in the same danger of dying. Only that that position exposes the truth about me whilst this position does not because I am not in the real world; it is a delusional world of mine. But those events in which there is real danger are good events because they reveal to us truly what is going on inside. This turmoil that is in here is the true state of me and you and many of us. What is happening is that we are projecting these insecurities upon everything we do, especially on our Islam and religion, its beliefs, rites and ceremonies.

The Prophet liberated a community, a frightened insecure community, who used to worship numerous Gods; who needed to make offerings and gestures to God and barter with God. The Prophet liberated them, gave them the reigns of their destiny, but as soon as he passed on they began to project these very insecurities on the values that the Prophet had left. It is the same thing that is happening today. Today, instead of making sacrifices to Lāt and ʿUzza, what do we do? We give charity (*ṣadaqa*) accompanied with the same sentiments of the pagan sacrifices. Have you ever considered the attitude with which we give charity? It is a very negative one at times. "O Allah, dispel all calamities from me." We are playing a game with Allah. This "God" that we are worshipping is akin to *Lāt* in the name of "God." Allah says, "If you give charity, I will prolong your life." I give charity out of fear for death. Allah says, "If you give charity, I will give you more." I make a bargain with God that I am giving this much, so give me this much back. Charity was meant to be an act performed selflessly for the sake of Allah and concern for others – and when performed selflessly for the sake of Allah it generates goodness, growth and evolution from within, and as that evolution is received from within, the world tends to such a heart. The world is a living being. It begins to yield to such a heart and begins to tweak herself in order to accommodate the safety of such an individual. But instead, my act of giving charity is a projection of my insecurities upon a very noble practice. Why do people solicit God's opinion through the practice of *istakhāra* when they are unsure of what to do? They have no confidence in making decisions. When the Prophet used to do *istakhāra* he would say, "I seek the best outcome from Allah, the same Allah who has intended bad for me, can re-intend good for me." That was *istakhāra*. "O Lord, whatever I am trying to do, make it the best for me." And the Lord says to Imam Ḥusayn, "I will kill you nonetheless." To this Ḥusayn opens his arms and says, "O Lord, I consider it the greatest honour." If you are finding all this strange, then please examine yourselves.

What happens on that night when in the morning we have to face the judgment of a lawsuit and our entire business empire could crumble? How do you feel that night? Do you lose sleep and your peace of mind? We can't eat. We can't even smile. By Allah this man who sleeps so restlessly at night, making bargains with Allah, praying the night-prayer (*namāz-e shab*) and doing this many glorifications (*tasbīḥ*) so that Allah may alleviate the difficulty, does he even know he is going to wake up in the morning alive? And if he wakes up in the morning, the same God who has looked after him in the womb of his mother, is He not capable of looking after him in his tomorrow? Allah invokes reason here and creates a rational framework for us to overcome these insecurities that are inborn within us and which we project onto religion. So we need to use reason as Allah says in the Quran. We need to address the inner insecurities.

Today in religion we have introduced practices that are wholly a projection of our inner fears and insecurities and have nothing to do with religion whatsoever, or either they are righteous activities of religion but the attitude with which they are performed is totally wrong. If people were to understand the meaning of substantive growth, of evolution from within, they would not need to pray a hundred-unit prayer. If only they understood that one sincere prostration can bring about such reliance on Allah that after that prostration they would no longer be fearful of the consequences of their destiny. That is better than a hundred units after which a person is still insecure.

All of these arduous and repetitive prayers we perform either become a ritual or they become expressions of our insecurity. They do not mean anything. They are prayers recited simply for the sake of reciting and for sake of repelling our insecurities. Seeking protection from Allah or seeking some gain from Allah has nothing to do with being God-centric. The same Islam which means surrender to Allah is not providing surrender to Allah. It is providing a tool for bargaining with God and hence there is no evolution or growth either at the individual level of the inner self or at the level of the many religious practices being performed and undiscerned – right from wrong. When we pray, the attitude is this: I have to pray this because it is obligatory (*wājib*). Does a person who prays so meticulously but with this frame of mind, tell me, have they become a better person? The answer is possibly no. It is here that we need to examine what we have done to our religion and what is happening to us. The way Allah modifies this is through reason, by establishing rational frameworks.

Allah says in the Quran, "There is no tribulation that will befall the Earth or you, but that I have already prescribed it in a book before I initiated the existence of the Earth so that you may not be overjoyed at what comes to you, you may not be over-grieved at what leaves you." (57:22-23) What does this mean? If we look at the example of Uḥud, people died. The people in Medina said, "If only they had not gone, they would not have died." Allah says, "In that case when death approaches you, repel it if you can. Nay when your death approaches, you will be dragged by your forelocks to the place where you are supposed to meet with your Lord, and you cannot do anything about it." (3:168; 3:154) So the people said, "Whatever that is bad is from the Prophet, and whatever good there is it is from Allah." Allah said, "Tell them Muḥammad, all of it is from Allah." (4:78) Allah is setting up rational parameters that invite us to look in this world of ours and realise that if we were to understand it very carefully we would know that we have the power of discernment at a very different level. Everything else is just planned. Our job is not to try and get control over anything. Our job is to do something else totally.

I will ask a series of questions, as the Imam asked his companion. Did any one of us choose the household into which we were born? Did any one of us choose our gender or our colour? Did any one of us choose our status? Has any one of us chosen the time of our death? The Imam puts these questions to the companion, "Have you chosen any of these things?" The companion says, "No." He says, "Then know that the choice is God's." This is what Allah says in the Quran, if you look at it very rationally. Life and death are not in your hands.

The religious people in their religion pray to God for long life, good health, wealth and victory over their enemy, and they do not see that the people who do not believe in their God have got better lives, more health, more wealth and the greatest glory in victory. Pharaoh, who says, "I am Allah!" Allah gives him the whole kingdom. Saddam, the biggest criminal, God gave him the whole of Iraq. Does this not bring a question to the mind: am I supposed to worship God for my sustenance? This is insecurity. A feeble mind says, "O Lord, I will pray to You tonight so you increase my sustenance." The angels laugh upon us. What if God were to give you millions but restricted your breath then what? How amazing is this story!? And what if God was to take the Sun out of the sky, then what? Do you not realise what you are saying? When we look at it this way we will say, "No, we need to understand things accurately." What God is saying in the Quran, think about it properly. Examine yourselves from within and examine your religions and set yourselves free. This is what God says in the Quran. When the prophets and angels understand this, they say, "You give life to whomsoever You want. You give death to whomsoever You want. You give sustenance to whomsoever You want. You take away sustenance from whomsoever You want.

You give humility to whomsoever You want. You give dignity to whomsoever You want. You give the kingdom to whomsoever You want and You snatch it away from whomsoever You want. You give wealth, and You give poverty." When we subscribe to this sort of an understanding what happens is that it sets us free fully from within and from false religious practices. Just imagine if a person were to understand that, "O Lord, You have created me. You have given me a lease of sixty to seventy years of life. I am not supposed to worry about sustenance, health and life. My task is to evolve, it is to come back to you". God-centricity and liberation. Imagine how productive that life would become. Imagine how productive that community would become. Imagine how glorious that religion would become. Think about it.

The Prophet's community was a suffocated community. It could not move. Illiteracy. Immorality. Lack of knowledge. Lack of enquiry. Lack of brotherhood. It was filled with warfare and totally devoid of human values. When the Prophet leaves them, see what they have become. How he breaks the inner and the outer shackles. He reforms them from within by making God the central tenet of their lives, and he reforms the religious beliefs and the social systems, and as soon as he does that everything is geared towards evolution and growth. Leave it to Allah. Grow as much as you can. If He wants to give sickness let Him. If he wants to give life let Him. And if He wants to take life and give death, let Him. My sole purpose is to evolve beyond all of this. This is what the Prophet did.

The religion of today, the religious practices of today, instead of being emancipating they are enslaving. This is supposed to be same Islam of the Prophet Muḥammad that allowed the Muslims to embrace the Jews and Christians in their state. In fact, history bears witness to this that when the Christian Crusaders went into Jerusalem, they murdered and massacred the Muslims and persecuted the Jews. When the Muslims were in Jerusalem they allowed for harmonious coexistence between all faiths. This is how liberated these people were. Today's Islam does what the pagans were doing.

In today's world, Allah Himself has become the point of enslaving. When Islam was brought to the prophetic society it was seen as an alternative to the pagan system. Today the very same pagan sentiments have come to be fashioned in the clothes of Islam so much so that we cannot see the alternative. So, this is what Allah says in the Quran. It's as if He is saying to us, "You need to understand that you are in this world, everything about this world is in My hand. Have the courage to change as much as you want. If you want to take the reins of your destiny into your hands, take it. You have no cause to be insecure." Allah says in the first few Sūrahs to the people of Medina who were fearful of death, He says to effect, "Go with this Prophet – if you were to die then you are coming to Me, is that not better?" What a simple question. "If you were to lose something, then I will give you far more, that is what you believe don't you? Why are you so frightened? Why are you so insecure? If you were to be wounded then I will be pleased with you. Is that not better for you?" He is removing their insecurities by giving them rational arguments. Then Allah says to those people in two other places, "If you are suffering, then they too are suffering at their loss, but at least you have hope of reward from Me that they do not have. Should that not make it easier for you to bear your sufferings?" (4:104) This was the way in which Allah reformed the community of the Prophet. He brought them out of insecurities and out of fears. He gave them utmost courage and belief. He empowered them, to the extent that these nomadic people stood at the greatest and the loftiest pedestal of human existence.

We need to ask this question of ourselves truly from within: Is my Islam giving me the opportunity to liberate myself? If I am true in my Islam and in my subscription to Allah, and in saying that I am the righteous one, then there is a litmus test – what if death were to befall me *right now*? Would I panic? Would I be searching for a doctor, or would I be so comfortable with my God that the same God that has accompanied me throughout my life is accompanying me at the point when I breathe my last, and the same God Who is accompanying me in my death will accompany me in my tomorrow in my grave and beyond my tomorrow. If I am that comfortable, then know that I am at the point of liberation through Islam, that my insecurities and fears have been absolved in my devotion and surrender to Allah, and I have truly come of age. If not, then my religion has not done anything for me.

Look at those beautiful moral agents that the Prophet created. You hear this all the time that the same people who used to kill each other at the mere fact that one person's horse preceded another's horse in drinking water. They would bear vendettas for generations. These very people at the battle of Uḥud, when one of them falls, the water bearer goes to him and he says to him, "There is one ahead of me, he is in more need of water." He runs to the second, the second sends him to the third, the third sends him back to the first, but the first has died. He rushes to the second, the second has died. He rushes to the third, and the third has died. The same people of yesterday, filled with insecurities, fears and arrogance, who would want to secure their own life at the mercy of everybody else's life are now giving life.

If you think what I am saying is strange, I am going to give an example of a conversation that took place last night. There is verse in the Quran – you have all read it. The verse says, "On that day a father shall flee from his son, a husband from his wife and a mother from her offspring, and they will say to Allah, 'throw them in the fire of hell. My mother, my father, my children, my wife, but save me from this hell.'" (70:11-13) So the questioner said, "What a pitiful day that will be, that we will say this." I said, "Really, will we say this? I certainly hope I don't say this." My God, what a pitiful state when I say to Allah, "Throw my mother in the fire, throw my wife in the fire." Why should I say this? But the Quran is saying this. But the Quran also includes the Prophet Muḥammad and ʿAlī ibn Abī Ṭālib. Do you think the Prophet would run away from ʿAlī ibn Abi Ṭālib? Do you think Imam ʿAlī would say, "Throw everybody into hell?" Can you see how we are reading things? We are not reading things accurately. If the Quran says this, it is probably talking about a group of people. The Quran also says, "I will admit them with their wives, with their parents, with their children into the folds of Paradise." (13:23) Why do you not read that as well? But this is the whole irrational attitude, a sign of the insecurities that we have. Now if a person knows that he is going to ask Allah to throw his mother in the pit of hell on the day of *qiyāmah*, how is he going to look at his mother in this world? Think about this. If a mother knows that these very children for whom I am sacrificing myself, I will ask Allah to "throw them in the pit of hell and save me," I am going to become that selfish. What sort of mother is this? The mother should question Allah, "O Lord, why would I say this?" And the preacher should be able to explain that, 'O dear woman, you will never do this.'

These insecurities, this lack of confidence, has plagued our understanding of religion. The whole attitude towards our religion has been messed up. We are introducing things in there, and the noble things that are in there are not being understood for the beautiful Godly worth they have. I will never ever say, God willing, "O Allah, throw these people inside hell." So these insecurities Allah conquers through reason. There is no need for you to fear from within. There is no need for you to transfer these fears upon your Islam. The most liberated man that we see is our Imam Ḥusayn. Look at the beautiful way in which he understands what is happening in Karbala. At one point he makes a prayer, he says, 'O Allah, if you have destined to withhold victory from me on this day..." What does that mean? It means Imam Ḥusayn went there seeking victory. Against all odds, he says, "O Lord, if you are with me, then anything is possible." And Ḥusayn more than anybody else knows the Quran, that when Ṭālūt took his group of people and when they were faced with Jālūt and his mighty army, the believers amongst the army of Ṭālūt said, 'How many a time has a small group been victorious upon a mighty group with the consent of Allah." Can you see that? This rational framework that Ḥusayn operated in was so empowering that even with his band of seventy-two people he said anything is possible, and the way he fought, he fought to kill and to win. A man does not fight in the way he fights to lose. Do you fight in such a battle to lose? You fight with such force because you know you want to conquer. In any case, when ʿAbbās falls, he states to Allah, "O Lord, if You have destined that You will withhold victory from me on this day…" It means that "O Lord, I am not going to be concerned with any of this. If You have destined I am going to die, then fine – I will die. But I will use it to come to You." He puts away all his fears.

This is what the *maqātil* – literature describing the events of Imam Ḥusayn's martyrdom – say. That he came three times when he was on his own to the tent of lady Zaynab and he looked at the enemy, thirty thousand swords. He is alone. He saw them and he cried out, "There is no might or strength save for that which is through Allah." This is the conviction of the man. He can do anything he wants at any point. I am not supposed to be a frightened individual. I am not going to pray to Allah to secure my life. There is no might greater than Allah's. This is how liberated this man is from within. At every death you find the state of his liberation growing. He is becoming a greater Godly soul than what he was before the fall of one of his men. But the men around Ḥusayn were handpicked, they were chosen for their calibre and their substance. Ḥurr, Muslim ibn Awsaja, Ḥabīb ibn Maẓāhir – these were no ordinary men. These were men of substance. Zuhayr ibn Qayn! Look at these people! It was the sheer God-centricity in these people that has allowed Karbala to live on. Can you imagine, Karbala is not even a dot on the map of the Earth and yet it is impacting human history so profoundly, to the extent that there is no country but that the mention of Ḥusayn is in that country. These were noble men, men of substance, men devoted to Allah, whose blood actually gave life to the decaying, dying veins of humanity. Ḥusayn's companions – each one of them – caused him utmost pain when they died, but he accepted their deaths because he was in a state of being totally surrendered to Allah. He was liberated. He was free.

Night Six

We stated earlier that we are insecure from within, and that this is a natural part of our psychology as we come into this world in the cradle of animality and begin to evolve. We are people who operate as imaginative children. As we grow we begin to reason, think accurately, and start to live a more fuller life. We begin to discern fact from fantasy and seek clarity. The philosophers similarly state that we need to have clarity of thought and question various claims. We need to discern what is factual from that which is fanciful. To give an example: the Hindus cremate their dead; the Muslims bury their dead; while the Parsi leave their dead out to be consumed. What we see as facts are bodies being cremated, bodies being buried, and bodies being consumed – this is the apparent fact. However, what we tend to do due to our emotional attachment with our own practices is that we attach negative values to religious and cultural practices that differ from ours. We are appalled at how the dead could be burned or left outside to be consumed by vultures. Now, if we were to look at it from the perspective of the Hindus, they would say that those cultures which bury their dead are people who are doing a disservice and disrespecting their deceased ones because the bodies will rot away and be consumed by insects in the Earth; they would be appalled at our practices. A philosopher reckons that whatever is outside your mind is a fact. The rest are assumptions driven by your emotions and/or imaginations.

They have no connection with the facts. For example, God has prohibited the consumption of pork and wine. Does this make the pig an ugly creature? This ugliness, this repulse, this inability to look at a pig, the pig becoming a swear word – these are constructs of the mind which are not *in* the factual world. Allah has created the pig for a purpose. The pig is a noble animal fulfilling an existential purpose intended by its creation. Allah clearly states that He has not created anything in vain. Therefore, if you hate or are disgusted by an animal that He has created you are actually pointing a finger at the creative work of Allah. Similar is the case of alcohol. Allah tells us not to consume it, but does this make alcohol ugly and repulsive? The philosopher tells us to think accurately, there is a reason why Allah has prohibited us from consuming alcohol. The emotional input is added by us and that needs to be checked.

There was once a Persian emperor who had conquered many lands. At one culture he found that the people consumed their dead and in another the people cremated their dead. So he asked both to bring their dead with their families to his court. He ordered the group that consumed their dead to cremate, and the people that cremated their dead to consume the body. Both were equally appalled. What he demonstrated was that the feelings of dislike have nothing to do with the apparent facts, but were merely a construct of their minds. To give another example: why do we get scared of being left alone with a dead body? What are we so afraid of? That poor dead person throughout his or her life was such a gentle person and now that he or she is dead and they are helpless, they cannot do anything. This is where reason needs to be used. We need to use our reason and sharpen our intellect to rid ourselves from insecurities and fears.

There are fears and insecurities within us that we bring from the cradle of animality. Religion asks for us to be liberated from these fears and insecurities through God-focus and God-centricity by totally surrendering to God. How does God construct this argument? He says death and life is from Me. If you, fearing death, try and gain control, you will not avert death. But you will lose your own freedom because then you will bow to every tyrant and whims of everyone else thereby becoming fully constricted and will not evolve. The Prophet of Allah said, "He who is afraid of other than Allah, Allah makes him fearful of all things." Darkness, spiders, sounds in the night, fear of loss and fear of death. Allah creates a very rational argument and says that the best way to overcome fear and insecurities is to embrace this fear by telling yourself that if Allah has destined this for me, then He is the best of planners. I pray to Allah to prolong my life but, O Lord, if you have decided otherwise for me then let me embrace Your destiny and free myself.

Human insecurities shape every individual's life, whether he is an atheist, believer or an agnostic. When we look at the world at large, we find it is based on fears and insecurities. Religion challenges this fear factor. Allah says, "You are proclaiming that you are returning to me so at that level you must embrace whatever I have destined for you. And if are able to do so you will release yourself of the fears and live as a free man." What we do instead is that we project an inner state of fear and insecurity on religious practices, which were noble existential principles designed to increase growth within us but as a result of our unfounded fears begin to curtail growth altogether. Take the practice of charity as an example. In a study conducted in America researchers found that people who give to charities voluntarily live longer. They found that giving stimulates the mesolimbic pathway, which is the reward centre of the brain, releasing endorphins and creating a happy feeling which calms the nervous system, reduces stress levels, and consequently prolongs life. These people were giving for the sake of giving. Their only motivation was to share their blessings as a pure and a noble act. What do some of us do? We give charity to dispel false fanciful fears. For example, whenever a black cat crosses my path I rush and give $20.00 in charity because I have constructed in my mind that this means bad luck. The non-Muslim who does not know of this will happily keep black cats, in the process taking much joy and pleasure from that. But I have made the black cat a point of insecurity; hence I give charity. This sort of charity becomes restrictive. To give charity is a beautiful facet of religion, but insecure people have projected their fears upon it and have deprived the act of giving its potency and its value. The intention should be that I am giving in order to gain the pleasure of Allah.

With regards to giving alms as means (*wasīla*) to Allah, if we are true in our claim that we are Muslims, and our source of religion is the Quran, the Prophet Muhammad, ʿAlī ibn Abī Ṭālib and the Imams, then we need to read the Quran, study the actions of these people to see what they understood by making "means." ʿAlī ibn Abī Ṭālib says in Duʿā al-Kumayl, which is one of the most wonderful supplications in its authenticity, content and eloquence, "I make You, my Lord, a means to You. I make You, O Lord, my means to Yourself." Ḥusayn ibn ʿAlī says, "I make my poverty a means to come to You. How can anything other than my poverty be a means to You?" We need to understand the meaning of seeking "means" through God-centricity, through the Quran, through the Prophet, through ʿAlī ibn Abī Ṭālib and through the sons of ʿAlī ibn Abī Ṭālib. Is this an irrational and unreasonable argument? Seeking means is a very elaborate understanding – when the Imams pray, "O Lord, I seek Your favours through Your name, through Your benevolence, through Your mercy, through Your Grace through Your kindness… I seek Your favours through Your handiwork: the heavens and Earth that You have created. I seek Your favours through Your chosen Prophet." In all of these prayers the Imams have focused only on God-centricity. It is all stemming through God. In every supplication they are focused on Allah. Through God-centricity they create every means. They are not seeing any agency independent or in isolation of God.

Imam Jaʿfar al-Ṣādiq advised, "When you promise your children anything, fulfil it because your children see you as their god. They will see you as a yardstick to estimate their god." In the beginning of life, we have means (*wasīla*) and we give those means independence, but as we mature Allah asks us to re-examine the whole issue of means and tells us to cut it all away. It is all through God. Nothing is independent of God. If a hand feeds you it's a means that Allah has supplied but not an independent means, otherwise it becomes a distraction. The whole focus of Islam was to bring God-centricity. To free the hearts and minds and bring them into the proximity of Allah. This means that when we become discerning adults we understand that there is nothing but that it is from Allah. Allah says to the Christians, "ʿĪsā and his mother, Maryam, eat and drink, don't you understand? (5:75) How can they be independent? They are wholly contingent to life, and I am the One Who supplies life and its demand to them." Allah says to the Christians in the Quran, "What if I were to destroy the Messiah and his mother? How can he be independent of Me? He is wholly contingent upon Me." (5:17; paraphrasing) And ʿĪsā himself declares, "I am a slave of Allah." (19:30) In other words, "I am wholly contingent upon Allah."

When the hypocrites of Uḥud said about those who were killed in the battle that if our brethren had stayed behind they would not have been killed, Allah responds to them by saying, "In that case repel death when it comes upon you. When death is destined for you, you will be dragged by your forelocks to the place where you are to die." (3:168; 3:154) They said, "O Muḥammad, we agree that all good is from Allah, but evil is from you." Allah replies, "Say everything is from Allah." (4:78) What they were actually saying was, "O Muḥammad, good as in life is from Allah; and since the decision to go to war was yours and it resulted in loss of lives, then evil is from you." Allah says, "No, everything is from Allah – sickness and health are both from Allah, defeat and victory are both from Allah." All that you can do is embrace your destiny and grow through it.

Muḥammad ʿAbdu had a dream and saw the blessed Prophet who said that the best thing that happened was the defeat in the battle of Uḥud because the Muslims were becoming complacent. They thought that Allah would grant them victory at all occasions, so in defeat they became more Godly whilst in victory they were becoming complacent, stagnated, regressive and arrogant. When Allah says, "Good is from Allah, evil is from you," (4:79) it means Allah only intends good and promotion of growth because He is the one who nurtures. "Evil is from you" refers to how we negatively interact with the situation.

When Ibrāhīm was being thrown in the fire, Gabriel trembled and implored Allah to save him. God gave him consent to go to Ibrāhīm.

Gabriel appeared and told him, "O Ibrāhīm, I can save you. Let me help you."

Ibrāhīm replies, "Gabriel, this is between me and my God, away with you."

Gabriel says, "In that case allow me to take your supplication to Allah and beg of Allah to save you."

Ibrāhīm replies, "He is aware of my state and He is needless of my prayer. If He wants He can burn me into ashes; if He wants He can keep me intact and cool the fire. I have embraced His decree?"

How wonderfully free this man is.

***

These beautiful facets of religion, the beautiful potent qualities of religion which were meant for our learning and growth, have become highly unproductive and distracting to the mind as we have projected our fears on them. Religion provides the rational framework within which Allah carries forward the individual to a newer pedestal of existence. He tells us to reason with everything. Discern between fact and what is the emotional input because of your fear and insecurity. If Allah has destined worldly failure for you and you embrace it as His will, then that is better than the success that takes you away from Allah. After many a fall does a child learn how to walk. If you never allow your child to fall they would never come of age. If Allah destines failure and if that brings inner success, then that is true success. You can become the king of this world, but if you have not found Allah then what have you found? You can be a road sweeper but if you have found Allah, what have you lost? The inner world is the true world of success and failure

So Allah tells us to go forth and achieve this lofty pedestal of existence, where reason yearns for a greater beginning. Even reason stops at a point and gives way to a loftier truth; the language of love knows no reason. If lady Zaynab had merely reasoned, would she have sent ʿAwn and Muḥammad to the battlefield? If John had simply reasoned with the situation would he have given his life to protect Ḥusayn with such passion? Here one sees that reason gives way to a loftier state of existence, since love knows no restraint when directed properly. Uways al-Qaranī breaks all his teeth in the love of the blessed Prophet. The Prophet did not condemn Uways because he was acting in the religion of love and said, "Indeed I smell the fragrance of the all-Merciful (*al-Raḥmān*) from the direction of Yemen." Reason itself brings the individual to the pedestal of love, and at this pedestal of love our reason gives way to a mystical vision of the Truth.

ʿUbayd Allah ibn Ziyād is poking at the face of Ḥusayn and he looks at Zaynab and says, "See what your God has destined for all of you?" This noble lady answers, "I have not seen anything but that the beauty of Allah prevails." Through which lens is Zaynab observing, I ask you? Do you not see Zaynab when she falls at the feet of Ḥusayn to stop him from going to the battlefield, and when he says, "The religion of our grandfather is being threatened," she says, "Go! if I had eighty Ḥusayn I would give them all." How is she understanding this?

On the day of Ashura, Zaynab was the one running to the battlefield to receive the bodies of the dead before any of the other women could get to their dead, but when the bodies of ʿAwn and Muḥammad were brought back, Zaynab was nowhere to be seen. She did not want her tears to cause embarrassment to her brother. But when Akbar fell, before Ḥusayn could drag himself to the body of Akbar, Zaynab was present knowing full well that the dagger embedded in the chest of Akbar would take the life of his father, so to speak, so she became the veil between Ḥusayn and his Akbar. This same Zainab after Ashura, her hands are tied behind her back and before her is the torn, beheaded body of her beloved brother, and she falls to the body and looks at the sky and says "O Lord, accept this offering." Reason itself gives way to a loftier pedestal of existence where pain and suffering becomes a means of increased Godliness. This mystical vision goes beyond reason – it has a language of its own where loss is gain, where death is life, poverty is wealth, sickness is health and defeat is victory.

When Mūsā appeared before the Pharaoh, he mocks at him. "Mūsā, look at your staff – all broken and cracked and old. Look at your clothes – could you not have adorned a more befitting attire? Indeed if you are from Allah, then where are your ranks of angels? Where are your riches?" That is how the Pharaoh reasoned, but Mūsā was in a state of his own. Mūsā has gone into the realm of Godliness. In a nutshell, when we allow reason to lead us to a greater status of existence, morality changes in the sense that motivation for being righteous changes. Reason dictates do good for the sake of good, not for the sake of gaining something. Love of God on the other hand dictates to us to do good to gain your Beloved God. Rabīʿa ʿAdawiyya would carry a bucket of water. When she was asked the reason she said, "In order to extinguish the fire of hell so that no one worships my Lord for fear of hell but they worship Him as He is worthy of worship." She cried out, "O Lord, if I have worshipped you for gaining paradise then deny it to me, and if I have worshipped you for fear of hell, then cast me therein." Do good for the sake of good and beyond to become godlike.

As Ḥusayn cries out, "O people! If you have no fear of the Hereafter and you have no care for the customs of the Arabs, at least be free men in this world of yours." There is a standard of good in itself, but there is a pedestal beyond it that is the lure of Allah, the lure of love, which burns the lover in Allah. The love of Allah, as Imam Ali says, does not pass over anything but it renders it into ashes. For this lover cannot withstand the beloved being at a distance. It is as if Ḥusayn said, "O Allah, I give You myself." Allah said, "I will take the chest of your Akbar." Ḥusayn said, "So be it." "I will take the arms of your ʿAbbās." Ḥusayn says, "So be it." "I will tear the neck of your Asghar." And his answer is, "So be it." "I will cause great hardship upon Sakīna." And Ḥusayn embraces it all. Morality reaches a pedestal where good is no longer just for the sake of doing good, but it is for the sake of becoming Godly; not only for the arbitrary proximity to God, but for the sake of displaying the beauty of God.

Who was the victor in Karbala? The one who lived or the one who was killed? Who was the greatest victor? The one who lost his two arms or the one who kept his two arms? The one who loses his two arms gains hands from Allah. These are the sequential stages of the evolution of the human soul through God-centricity. Allah says, "We are Allah's and we are returning to Allah." (2:156) This statement means that we lose ourselves fully so as to arrive at that divine pedestal of existence.

Ibrāhīm took a mighty leap of faith going against his reason in sheer passion of Allah. The "Ibrāhīm" of Karbala displayed the noble substance of his grandfather, the friend of God. A mother will sacrifice her sleep for the wellbeing of her children. She will go hungry to feed her children. A mother is one who lives and dies for her children. So how do we explain the mothers of Karbala who are spurring their children to death? They are in a different realm. They do not reason like me and you. Their hearts are filled with love. The object of their love is Ḥusayn ibn ʿAlī. These are the mothers of Karbala. They are on that level of God-centricity. God liberates us through reason from our insecurities and fears. As free men, we are lead to God through the sword of reason and as we become God-centric, reason gives way to a mystical vision where God-centricity culminates in total immersion in the splendour and the will of God.

Night Seven

We stated that in the whole process of human liberation, God-centricity and surrender to Allah, reason plays a pivotal role. Allah invokes reason and constantly encourages the human being to think, to determine what makes sense as opposed to what does not. This results in dispelling fears and false beliefs and the human being swiftly begins to grow. This state gives way to a state of centricity that brings about a close intimate bond with Allah, a state where Allah is enough for a person.

In order to achieve this, there has to be an agent that shows us how to live through Allah, through God-centricity, through fluidity; who demonstrates to us how surrender works and how we can evolve through that surrender to Allah. For this we are told to follow the model of the blessed Prophet, which means that the Prophet has to be somebody who can be followed. It would be wholly unjust to confine the model of the Prophet to his external being only. "External being" means in terms of his actions without looking at the substance and the essence through which those actions are resulting. This is one position within the faithful community that if they get this right, they will understand Islam most accurately, and Islam would then be able to produce, be productive and bring about wholesome, productive human beings. If we can understand what it means to follow a Prophet, a living example who has to be exactly like you and me, and through the weaknesses and the frailties that you and me have, then that example can show us how we can become Godly, how we can grow from the utmost state of weakness into a state of great strength – from a state of insecurity to a state of confidence; from a state of relying upon the world, to a state of God-centricity and reliance upon Allah. If this were not the case, they would not be deemed appropriate models. The huge success Prophet Muḥammad had was because he questioned the status quo. He stated that these things do not make sense. He suffered the way we suffer. He felt the same fears and anxieties as we do, but through that he lived such a righteous life. He reconciled these weaknesses into such Godliness and Godly strength that this is what deems him a suitable role model for all of humanity. On the other hand, Prophet ʿĪsā, the impeccable prophet of Allah born without a father, speaking in his cradle loses the right to be a model for us because of our inability to relate to him due to his miraculous birth. The huge success of the blessed Prophet was that he lived through Godliness within the human context. He was *human* to the core. In the Quran the prophets declare their humanity and Allah does not shy away from talking about the frailties of their humanity, and how they reconciled those weaknesses and frailties within divinity and Godliness. If the Prophet did not have these qualities, he would not be a worthy example for us.

The believing community entertains certain ideas that are inconsistent with the Quran and the model of the Prophet. From there they deduce a belief structure that takes away the true understanding of the Prophet, the real Islam, and the correct method of how to conduct our journey towards Allah. The very fact that the Companions followed the Prophet was because they could relate to him as a human being. They said he is one like us and if he can live such a righteous life, so can we. He was accessible in that way. The ideas that we have are that the Prophet had to be the best at everything. Let us try and unravel this. For example, Gabriel used to come to the Prophet in the form of a handsome man. Imam ʿAlī was with the Prophet when he was receiving the revelation. When the Prophet declared his prophethood, Imam ʿAlī was still a young man. When the Prophet was fifty years old,

Imam ʿAlī was a grown man. When Gabriel came to the Prophet in the most handsome form, he did not come in the form of Imam ʿAlī. So now, according to our estimation, the most handsome man ought to have been Imam ʿAlī after the Prophet. Can you see the inaccuracy in our thinking? How are we understanding the notion of the Prophet and the Imams as role models? The way we reason is inconsistent with the facts and realities as they stand. The naive theological position that we have taken is that the Prophet has to be the best at everything. Of course he has to be the best but what is the meaning of "the best"? Does it mean the best shaped nose, the best runner, the best cricketer? The best business man? What is this best?

The spirit of God, ʿĪsā, was born without a father and he spoke in his cradle. Prophet Muḥammad *had* a father and did *not* speak from the cradle. Yet he has a loftier position! So what has made him better than ʿĪsā? Allah says about Prophet Mūsā, "From the very beginning, We caused him to refuse the breast of [Egyptian] nurses; and [when his sister came to know this] she said: 'Shall I guide you to a family that might rear him for you, and look after him with good will?' And thus We returned him to his mother, so that her eye might be gladdened, and that she might grieve no longer, and that she might know that God's promise always comes true – even though most of them know it not." (28:13). From this we create a theology that the milk of a non-believer is prohibited (*ḥarām*) upon a prophet. We know that our blessed Prophet's wet nurse was Ḥalīma, yet Islam had not come at that point. But he drinks her milk and he is the best Prophet.

There are many assumptions that need to be re-examined. We have created theologies that are inconsistent with the teachings of the Quran. There are many areas of history that need to be understood correctly. We need to be open and objective at the rational level. The attitude that we need to acquire is that of the companion of the Prophet before he came to be officially recognised as a "Companion." When the Prophet came to them they had no assumptions; they listened and weighed what he had to say with their reason. For them it was not *who* was conveying the Message, but *what* was being conveyed that mattered. For example, if we were to listen to a sermon by a man with a long grey beard, a turban and flowing robe, we would pay attention to what he was saying. The form and attire give us a sense of security that whatever he is saying is true. But if the same man was to wear a suit and tie, we would question everything he was saying. Why do we give labels? Why do the worth of the words being conveyed not carry independent value? To give another example, if portions of the Bhagavad Gita were included in the Quran we would all believe it, but if there are portions of what is mentioned in the Quran in the Bhagavad Gita, we will disbelieve it. This is where we are going wrong. Let us begin to think. Hear the words for what they are meant.

When we look at the Holy Prophet, the best of human beings and our role model, we are failing to understand what it means to be a role model. Loss is when people stop thinking; when people cannot see the words for what they mean. Allah says in the Quran:

> *Behold, God does not disdain to propound a parable of a gnat, or of something [even] less than that. Now, as for those who have attained to faith, they know that it is the truth from their Sustainer – whereas those who are bent on denying the truth say, "What could God mean by this parable?" In this way does He cause many a one to go astray, just as He guides many a one aright: but none does He cause thereby to go astray save the iniquitous.* (2:26)

Those with corruption in their hearts will say, "What does Allah mean by this example?" And in another verse He says, "He it is Who shows you His wonders [in all nature], and sends down sustenance for you from the sky: but none bethinks himself [thereof] save those who are wont to turn to God" (40:13). Again, in another verse He says:

> *In matters of faith, He has ordained for you that which He had enjoined upon Noah – and into which We gave thee [O Muhammad] insight through revelation as well as that which We had enjoined upon Abraham, and Moses, and Jesus: Steadfastly uphold the [true] faith, and do not break up your unity therein. [And even though] that [unity of faith] to which thou callest them appears oppressive to those who are wont to ascribe to other beings or forces a share in His divinity, God draws unto Himself everyone who is willing, and guides unto Himself everyone who have yearning hearts for the truth.* (42:13)

Every statement can be taken in two ways. Those with inner corruption are lead astray even through the verses and revelation. As the Quran says: "He guides through the verses those who desire and yearn Him." For the sake of Allah, if we are gathered here to talk about the most liberated man, Ḥusayn ibn ʿAlī, then let's listen with liberated minds. With regards to the Prophet of Allah, we are more interested in knowing how he prayed, how he sat, what he ate, how he prayed. We do not want to know the essence of Muḥammad, the Messenger of Allah. We will eat with two fingers and a thumb because that is how the Prophet ate, but we do not see that he did not cheat anybody to acquire the food that he was eating.

Imam Jaʿfar al-Ṣādiq asked Abū Ḥanīfa about how the Prophet ate. He replied, "With two fingers and a thumb." The Imam said, "You do not know how to eat." Abū Ḥanīfa asked him what he meant. The Imam replied, "Before you eat with two fingers and a thumb, observe the prophetic model – which is not just that what you eat is lawful in terms of permissible (*ḥalāl*) and impermissible (*ḥarām*), but in terms that you have not consumed anybody else's wealth unjustly." That was the real model of the Prophet of Islam. The Imam said, "If you have consumed that which is wholesome, then whether you consume with a whole fist or with two fingers it does not make a difference." If you are consuming that which is not wholesome then what difference does it make how you eat? It is wrong no matter how much formal Islamic eating etiquette you observe. If you cut the head of Ḥusayn, the best man, what difference does it make if after that you say "In the Name of Allah" and pray!? In fact, the model of the Prophet was something incredibly lofty. He was a role model who could be followed by the people because he was one like us. Just like every other prophet before him, he was one like us. When the Prophet saw danger and Allah said, "Muḥammad stand your ground," the real model of Muḥammad was such that he stood in front of the impending danger and said, "There is no power or might save through Allah." That resolve in Muḥammad is the real model of the Prophet: as one who is God-centric. He is so reliant on Allah. He says to himself, "If this is what my God wants, this is what I will do."

The model of the Prophet was such that if something was taken away from him, he says, "To God we belong and to Him we return." If Allah has destined it to go, then let it go. When Ibrāhīm died in his lap, he said, "O child, even as the eyes tear and my heart is torn apart, my tongue shall not utter anything which is displeasing to my Lord nor inconsistent with the decree of the Most Merciful." That is the model of Muḥammad. When he would travel, he would pray, "O Allah, I leave my family behind, but I leave with this certainty that as you have been caring for them in my presence, by priority you will care for them in my absence." That is the true model of the Prophet. His God-centricity went beyond reason where reason gives way to Godliness.

What are these prophets? Read the Quran accurately and you will see that each one of them displays their humanity, their humanness, and their human frailties. Each one of them is evolving. In the example of Ibrāhīm, we see him evolving gradually as he evolves from a prophet (*nabī*) to a messenger (*rasūl*) to a friend of God (*khalīl*) and finally to an *imām*. Gradual process of evolution, gradual process of coming to age, gradual process through surrender and God centricity, gradual process of liberation of Ibrāhīm until he comes to the fullness of his being. Ibrāhīm asks: "O my Sustainer! Show me how You give life to the dead." Said He:

"Do you not have faith?" (Abraham) answered: "I do, but [let me see it] so that my heart may be set fully at rest." (2:260) This verse shows that there is something beyond rational faith. I want that certitude to touch me from within. "Said He: 'Take, then, four birds and teach them to obey you. Then place them separately on every hill [around you]. Then summon them: they will come flying to you. And know that God is almighty, wise." (2:260) Then we see again in another *sūrah*: "And thus We gave Abraham [his first] insight into [God's] mighty dominion over the heavens and the Earth – and [this] to the end that he might become one of those who are inwardly sure." (6:75) These are evolutionary stages that Ibrāhīm goes through, one after another. Ibrāhīm is evolving. His restrictions are being loosened. He is breaking through the self-imposed insecurities, self-imposed limits. He is breaking through with surrender and God-centricity. When he puts his son Ismāʿīl under the blade, that is finally when Allah removes all veils.

Look at Prophet Mūsā. He says:

> *And when Moses came [to Mount Sinai] at the time set by Us, and his Sustainer spoke unto him, he said: "O my Sustainer! Show [Thyself] unto me, so that I might behold Thee!" Said [God]: "Never canst thou see Me. However, behold this mountain: if it remains firm in its place, then – only then – wilt thou see Me. And as soon as his Sustainer revealed His glory to the mountain, He caused it to crumble to dust; and Moses fell in a swoon. And when he came to himself, he said: "Limitless art Thou in Thy glory! Unto Thee do I turn in repentance; and I shall [always] be the first to believe in Thee!* (7:143)

He is fully displaying his humanness and wanting to grow through brutal honesty. Look at how he displays his humanness unashamedly when he returns to find his people gone astray:

> *And when Moses returned to his people, full of wrath and sorrow, he exclaimed: "Vile is the course which you have followed in my absence! Have you forsaken your Sustainer's command-*

ment?" And he threw down the tablets [of the Law], and seized his brother's head, dragging him towards himself. Cried Aaron: "O my mother's son! Behold, the people brought me low and almost slew me: so let not mine enemies rejoice at my affliction, and count me not among the evildoing folk!" (7:150)

Each and every one of them is human. They have their humanity at the core of their being. It is how they reconciled the weakness of their humanity and frailty in Godliness that makes them champion role models.

Look at Prophet Nūḥ – how he imprecates as a human who has lost hope in his people: "And Noah prayed: "O my Sustainer! Leave not on Earthy any of those who deny the truth. For, behold, if you do leave them, they will [always try to] lead astray those who worship You, and will give birth to nothing but wickedness and stubborn ingratitude." (71:27)

They are every bit human, but it is how they reconcile that human weakness and grow through it that makes them the special people they are. Look at the examples of Sāra and Hājara, the wives of Ibrāhīm, who demonstrate their emotional states. Both are mothers of grand prophets, yet Sāra is filled with such jealousy at Hājara giving birth that she drives her to a distant land and demands Ibrāhīm to leave her. The angels come to Sāra and say, "Allah will give you a child called Isḥāq." Despite the human frailty, she is worthy of carrying Isḥāq in her womb. When Ibrāhīm was leaving Hājara and the baby, Hājara calls out to him, "We will die in the scorching heat. Why are you leaving us in this scorching heat?" They are showing their humanness. They are human to the core. There is something profound in them which we have to understand. Prophet Nūḥ had said a few things and Prophet Muḥammad is told to repeat these: "Say [O Prophet]: "I do not say unto you, 'God's treasures are with me'; nor [do I say], 'I know the things that are beyond the reach of human perception'; nor do I say unto you, 'Behold, I am an angel': I but follow what is revealed to me." Say: "Can the blind and the seeing be deemed equal? Will you not, then, take thought?" (6:50). When Imam Ḥasan runs after Imam ʿAlī, "O father, do not go to the mosque. They will kill you!" Imam ʿAlī replies with the verses from Sūrah Luqmān: "and no one knows in what land he will die, Verily. God [alone] is all-knowing, all-aware." (31:34) The final destiny is in the hands of Allah, only He knows. Observe how Imam ʿAlī is humbling himself – that is what makes them into role models, this state of not knowing and still being Godly.

The Holy Quran reports the Prophet saying in Sūrah al-Aʿrāf: "Say [O Prophet]: "It is not within my power to bring benefit to, or avert harm from, myself, except as God may please. And if I knew that which is beyond the reach of human perception, abundant good fortune-would surely have fallen to my lot, and no evil would ever have touched me. I am nothing but a warner, and a herald of glad tidings unto people who will believe." (7:188) At the same time the Prophet says that Abū Lahab shall perish, and it happens. When he says, "The Romans have been conquered" he is talking about matter of the unseen (*ghayb*). At one point he is saying he does not know the *ghayb*, so we need to qualify things properly. Try and understand these great personalities whom Allah has appointed as role models for us instead of creating your own fanciful ideas around them making them unworthy of being followed.

The Prophet says in the Quran: "I do not know what is going to be done to me or to you." (46:9) Only Allah has the final say. Here is a role model who suffers like you, pains like you, has anxieties like you, but in his own anxiety he does not fall from the pedestal of righteousness; in that fear he does not lack the resolve and the courage. Allah is showing us his humanity. How many times Allah says to the Holy Prophet that you are My Messenger, you are indeed My Messenger. On many occasions in the Quran, Allah consoles the Holy Prophet who is experiencing human sentiments and emotions. He is human to the core; but the beauty about him is that he is so God-focused that he does not go against the good pleasure of his Lord. This is the beauty of the Prophet. When the community abandons reading the Quran, all other theologies creep in. The Prophet said, "Anything that is attributed to me, check it against the Quran." Imam ʿAlī and all the Imams have said that the Book of Allah is the yard stick. Look at the exemplary life of the Messenger of Allah. We are told in the Quran: "Say [O Prophet]: 'If you love God, follow me, [and] God will love you and forgive your sins; for God is much-forgiving, a dispenser of grace." (3:31) It begins with you and ends with you.

On the Marwa mountain the Prophet said to the people of Quraysh, "If you come to me on the day of *qiyāmah* and you are not righteous, I will not be able to do anything for you. And if a slave who is not noble in your sight were to come as a righteous person, he will get salvation and I will be able to do something for him." Other than God, righteous deeds, and *qiyāmah*, there is nothing in the story of salvation. Live a life that is God-centric.

The Quran says: "Verily, in the Apostle of God you have a prime example for everyone who looks forward [with hope and awe] to God and the Last Day, and remembers God unceasingly." (33:21). The Prophet is an example – a model before you so that you can learn how to lead a Godly life. The Prophet is being told by Allah in a variety of verses that, "O Muḥammad, We may either show you what We have promised them, or we may kill you before that." (40:77) How amazing is this? That God leaves the Prophet in such uncertainty, not giving him any reassurance. "We may give you victory, We may not." What sort of verses are these? These verses are testing the metal of the Prophet and showing us that even with such uncertainty about his future, the Prophet remains righteous to the end. He is righteous in the moment. I do not know what will happen, but in this moment I will only do what Allah requires me to do.

Every reformer and every prophet has been rejected by the majority. Every reformer has been met with opposition. The opposition has been irrational and emotionally based. How can we leave our forefathers? How can we leave our Gods? Consider the verse: "And convey unto them the story of Noah – when he said unto his people: "O my people! If my presence [among you] and my announcement of God's messages are repugnant to you – well, in God have I placed my trust. Decide, then, upon what you are going to do [against me], and [call to your aid] those beings to whom you ascribe a share in God's divinity; and once you have chosen your course of action, let no hesitation deflect you from it; and then carry out against me [whatever you may have decided], and give me no respite!" (10:71). Every prophet has been rejected. Our Prophet was driven out of Mecca. This is what happens to reformers because reformers will point to that which is factual and true. Every time something fanciful is being said, the person proclaiming the fanciful idea will have to go to great lengths to prove his argument. However, that which is factual does not need much persuasion since it will be rationally based. The Prophet is a reformer *par excellence*. His substance can be seen with this example: he is sitting on the back of a camel and a whole *sūrah* is revealed to him (i.e. Sūrah al-Anʿām). This is when the Meccans were antagonizing him to the peak and this was at a time when he lost his pillar of support, Abū Ṭālib, and his beloved wife, Khadīja. So, the Meccans had a free hand and were antagonizing him. Sūrah al-Anʿām was revealed in one continuous revelation without interruptions. Now if you read Sūrah al-Anʿām, you find that this *sūrah* is most forceful in challenging and dismantling and breaking all the beliefs and corrupt social systems of the Meccans. Allah reasons that if these people are forceful against you, I will make you even more forceful, shatter them in one go. If they want to kill you, let them kill you; but I will not let you back off. Any reasonable mind would say "be diplomatic, back off," "reason with them," "bow down to them," "become clever with your words." But the Quran is emphatic – never before had the Quran been so emphatic and forceful. The Prophet is constantly being told, "Say! Say!" Never has the command "Say!" been repeated so many times in any other *ṣūrah*: "Muḥammad say…" "Muḥammad say…" "Don't back off, hold your ground, and say it." "I know what I am doing," says Allah. Any human mind would want to relent just a little, but the Prophet is being pushed. To be in that position and to have the resolve to do the right thing and to convey the truth against all odds is what makes Muḥammad, Muḥammad. And it is this resolve that made Ḥusayn, Ḥusayn – the father of free men. That is why *ūlū l-ʿazam* (literally, "possessors of great resolve") are known as the *crème de la crème* of the prophets. *Ūlū l-ʿazam* is their resolve: they are human to the core yet they arrive at such a pedestal of Godliness that they acquire the strength which makes them steadfast so as to make even the mountains move and shake. This is not by miracles but by their human substance. In pursuit of God this is what they have become. In their surrender to God and Islam. In their God-centricity they have been liberated to this extent that even if I am shot down by arrows, I will convey the truth no matter what.

Sūrah al-Qiyāmah is one of the earlier Meccan *sūrahs* in which the Prophet is described as desperately trying to have everything recorded so that nothing is forgotten. Allah reminds him that his duty is to only follow the Message and convey the Message as commanded by Allah. This explains the human state of the Prophet when the earlier revelation was being received by him. He is a model not by miraculous attributes. The Prophet is a model through his concrete humanness, through how he has surrendered to God so awesomely in which God has taken him from pedestal to pedestal of human existence. The Messenger of Allah did not have a miraculous birth, nor did he speak from the cradle, nor had he turned the fire into garden, nor had he split apart the River Nile. He is the champion of all the prophets through his humanness and his human calibre and his God-centricity. We find this beautiful substance of the Holy Prophet displayed in ʿAlī, Ḥasan and Ḥusayn. The resolve of Imam Ḥusayn is shown on the day of Ashura when he cries out: "By Allah, you will never face a man fiercer than me in defeating falsehood." He is cut into pieces yet he refuses to surrender. Look at this great man. Everything that can go wrong with a person is happening to him: the fear of losing your children; the fear of captivity of your womenfolk. Look at his status of dignity: the man is calm; there is serenity about him; the man is righteous. Observe the level of his spirituality. If Ḥurr had come to me or to you, what would you do? I would say, "O Ḥurr, looking at you offends me – go away. Had it not been for you, I would not have been trapped in this situation. What difference does it make to me whether you join me or fight against me?" But observe the response of Ḥusayn. Look at the peak of Ḥusayn's morality and righteousness. He says "O Ḥurr, you are a friend of God right now and no longer a sinner," and he embraces him. He does not lose sense of righteousness. This is what a role model is.

Night Eight

In terms of our theme, "Islam, God-centricity and Human Liberation," we have stated that the role models provided in the form of the blessed prophets of Allah and the Imams He has sent were accurate role models for us to emulate. They had to be like us within our human context. They had to suffer. They had to feel pain. They had fears and anxieties like we do. But despite that, the God-centricity they had saved them from falling from the lofty pedestals of righteousness and instead brought them to a position where these weaknesses turned into strengths. They reconcile frailties in divine strength – this is why they are accurate role models. One of the essentialities of this is that they do not have absolute knowledge of what was going to happen. If that were the case then they would not have served as useful role models and we would not be able to emulate them accurately. In addition, it gives way to a lot of fanciful theology which does not belong in religion, and which has clouded our religion totally.

These great people were thinking beings. They challenged the status quo of their time, and because of this they were chastised. But their commitment to Allah and their resolve was such that they fearlessly delivered the message by questioning every assumption held by the people to whom they were sent. In addition, they lived by those noble human truths in a way that people could relate to them and take comfort that if somebody like him can be so righteous, despite suffering the way I am suffering or more so, without any miraculous godly powers that we attribute to superhuman characters, then I can do the same myself. This is the reason why the Prophet of Islam was so successful in giving salvation to his community. From a community of warring people, illiterate, burying daughters, sacrificing children to their gods, superstitious, insecure, petty, exploitive people who rejoiced in human tragedy and created human tragedy. These very people within twenty years are transformed to an extent that Allah praises them: "You are the best of people that have been produced within mankind." (3:110)

Consider from where to where? Allah says about them, "You were on the brink of falling into the fire of hell had Allah not sent His Messenger to save you." (3:103) From that position, to a position where Allah is praising them and calling them the best of people produced within mankind. How did the Prophet achieve this? By being human to the core. By challenging all that was contrary to human growth and evolution, and by living a godly life and never moving away from the course of righteousness. People observed this, they took comfort in this, they followed his example, and as a result they were liberated. So what was the message that the Prophet of Allah gave to them? What did the Prophet do? What did he do in terms of his teaching? This is the fundamental point that we need to ask. What were the shackles that he broke? What were the weights that they were carrying upon their shoulders that pinned them to the ground? The weights and shackles were their *false* beliefs and *false* cultures. The Prophet lifted off the baggage, the historical baggage that had accumulated in their heads, and this baggage is not a baggage specific to the pagans of Mecca – it is human baggage. Do you not see the believer (*muʾmin*) among the ranks of that despot Pharaoh? When he speaks to the Pharaoh about Prophet Mūsā and Harun and says, "He has come to you. You had said after Yusuf nobody would come." (40:28-44) This means that they understood the message of Yusuf, but after Yusuf went and prior to Mūsā's coming the Egyptians started placing the baggage of false beliefs through human insecurity into religion until it became so convoluted that Pharaoh was seen as a god. When religion moves away from its core teachings, what happens? We revert to our former ways and add to the religion. What was the baggage that the Prophet was removing and what was he giving instead? This is a fundamental question that everybody needs to ask.

Islam is our heritage. We are Muslims. But what is Islam? Religion can never be based on signs – it has to be based on reason. Beyond that it needs to be based on a spiritual devotion to Allah. Few years back we saw videos of Ganapati (elephant God of the Hindus) consuming milk, and this was taken as a sign of the validity of Hinduism. It is strange isn't it that the people see the Bhagwān drinking milk and they say, "Right, Hinduism is true." Then you saw devotees bleeding from the palm of their hands during Easter – stigmata – and this was a sign that Christianity must be true. The amazing thing is that Jesus didn't even go onto the crucifix, and still the palms bleed. If you are indeed open-minded people with sincere hearts for Allah then listen to this: when the prayer beads (*tasbīḥ*) turn red on the day of Ashura, does that then mean that the whole of Shiism is true? Therefore, by that reasoning, Hinduism is true as well; Christianity is true as well. These were the things that were added to religion. Religion became *other* than religion. It was strictly supposed to be based on right and wrong. As human beings we should not be distracted by these signs. Yesterday I saw people who would not cross the road because a black cat crossed there. Which chapter (*sūrah*) or verse (*āya*) in the Quran talks about a black cat? And then you have people who get frightened when they encounter a black crow. But Allah says there is no might or strength greater than Him. Where does the fear of the crow come from? On a lighter note, the black cat and the crow are the biggest mercy of Allah because they induce people to quickly give charity (*ṣadaqa*). At least their fear is propelling them to give to the poor which they may not do otherwise. So, what was the Prophet doing? The Prophet was breaking every *false* notion and idea that was added to religion. He was giving confidence to human beings. He was saying, "If a crow determines your destiny, then throw a stone at the crow and re-determine your own destiny." So the symbol, the metaphorical meaning there is that if the crow is destining something evil for you, then you re-destine it by throwing a stone at the crow.

This is what the Prophet did: he cut through superstitions and false beliefs. He said, "This is wrong. Let Allah be your only focus. Be God-centric." He empowered people and gave them the courage to take the reins of destiny into their own hands, to destroy all the gods that they had created through their own insecurities. So now I ask, "O Messenger of Allah, what have you given in place of breaking all of this?" The answer is clear: the Quran!

If you look at the Quran, you will find that the majority of its verses are about the nature of God and God-world relationship. They talk about God and His relationship with the human being; the purpose of the human being; and of moral existence. They talk about how a human being ought to be and this is explained through anecdotes and stories. Of these 6,200 verses or so, five hundred, in a very ambiguous manner, are about the laws of Islam and the *fiqh* of Islam. Why is this? Think about it: why is the Quran like this? Why is it then that the law portion is so small and so insignificant within the Quran? The reason is simple: because the whole purpose was to understand God, God-centricity, and to become God-like through actualising those fine Godly human traits within us; that was the whole purpose. That was the essence of religion. That is what the entire religion (*dīn*) is all about. Law was not issued for the sake of the law; law was issued for the sake of us becoming moral and spiritual beings. As Aristotle and Plato stated, the only function of the mechanism of law was to make us moral. It is an intermediary. It can fluctuate and change. That has been the salient principle in *every* religion. Why does the Prophet say, "I believe in everything revealed to me, and everything revealed to the people of the Book – referring to the Jews and Christians"? If the religions were not the same in essence, why did the Prophet say I believe in everything revealed to us and everything revealed to you? The Prophet did not practice the Rabbinic Law of the Jews, so why is he saying this? The only reason he said that is because all religions are *one* religion. If you look at the word *islām* within the Quran and look at the deliberations of the likes of Ṭabāṭabāʾī, he says, "There has only been one religion that has been fashioned differently from time to time." The law mechanism is only there to fashion the morals of a society in a given context.

The reason why Judaism was replaced by Christianity and Christianity by Islam is not because the essence of religion was faltering. It was not replaced in essence – it was replaced in *form* to bring back the essence that had been forgotten. *The essence has been the same*. What does this show? It shows that the human community evolves, and as it grows the same moral teachings need to be fashioned and refashioned. It is an evolutionary track. We are all growing. Something that is good for a child and acceptable from a child's perspective is unacceptable from the perspective of a fully-grown man. If a child were to run in a mosque we would accept it, but if a grown man was to start running around it would not be acceptable. The same facet of growth is fashioned differently. So the *form* of the law keeps on changing even though the essence stays the same, and this is the whole secret of the Prophetic message. He gave confidence to his community and empowered them. He stated, "Quran is minimalistic in terms of laws. Islam is minimalistic in terms of laws." Find me detailed examples of the laws of marriage – they are absolutely minimal. Contract laws are absolutely minimal. Why? Because there was not supposed to be a hard and fast system that gives laws perfectly until the end of time. When the Imam says, "*Ḥalāl* of Muḥammad is *ḥalāl* for all time; ḥarām of Muḥammad is ḥarām for all time," nobody can deny that. But the forms may change, and the Quran is full of examples of the forms changing. The other thing to bear in mind is that when the Quran gave a law it had to be given in a context in accordance with the strengths and weakness of the people. For example, the verse in Sūrah al-Nūr about a woman's covering (*ḥijāb*), the verse which states, "Let them draw their flaps upon their bosoms," it is only saying that because women at the time, when the verse was being revealed, wore turban-like headgear with flaps. If they did not have headgear with flaps that verse would not have been phrased the way that it is phrased. Look at the other verses of the Quran: you will see that it has to be within the prevalent context when it is supplying its laws and fashioning its morality. It can't be otherwise. To explain this point further, we do not find an apple or a kangaroo mentioned in the Quran, yet the theological assumption is that there is nothing in the world except that it is mentioned in the Quran. The minds are naive.

The Quran itself is restricted in the way it can speak in terms of the language and the examples it gives. So, when the Quran talks about two female witnesses as opposed to one male witness – that if you cannot find two men then bring one man and two women so that if one forgets the other one can remind her – it does not say principally two. In the context in which this verse was revealed, the women were not educated and therefore not accustomed to making rational decisions or retaining information. At an intellectual level they were kept in a protective child-like state. Therefore, the Quran had to address the people according to their strengths and weaknesses. As one of the students of Ayatollah Muṭahharī said, "The Quran did not come to fully conclude the discussion on human rights or female rights – it merely initiated the discussion." Similarly, the whole notion of slavery. The Quran institutionalized mechanisms to bring slavery to an end yet it did not decisively end it. Slavery is no longer being practiced in the modern world – if it is practiced, it is done secretively as it is considered unacceptable by society. So, the laws in the Quran are minimal and the reason for that is because the major theme is re-instilling morality and to become God-like.

Through this system how did the Prophet liberate his people? Consider this: had the blessed Prophet said that there is a law for everything even the way you sneeze, the minds of the community would have become dormant. On the contrary, the Prophet put the burden of responsibility on the people. He said, "These are the principles and here are the laws in broad which you need to understand in your own contexts and take your own decisions." So they, the Companions of the Prophet, would make decisions based on the morality and the broad parameters of the Quran, as opposed to the pagans who made themselves so constricted by their self-created gods. The previous pagans could not make any transactions without first making a sacrifice to their idols. In place of that the Prophet said, "No, you are the divine agency here. These are the laws. Take them and evolve." Through the teachings of the Quran the Prophet took the little community of warring people to a league of nations; from blood-thirsty people to a nation who were embracing the Jews, the Christians, Sabians and Hindus alike. He frees them and gives them discretion – this discretionary area has to always be present minus the religious baggage that we imposed in the name of religion. How is the world evolving? From feudalism to communism to capitalism. How can there be evolution if there are fixed laws within which we must operate? The only thing that has been happening in this social evolution is that there should be "fairness." This fairness at one point is garmented with feudalism, at another point with communism, and then again later with capitalism. The Prophet brought a minimalistic law-based religion which reminded people of the loftier truths of theology, of the loftiest pedestal of morality that they should acquire. "This is how you get to Allah. Here are the parameters, now you go and choose what is right and wrong." He gave discretion to the human being to decide between right and wrong.

We constantly have debates from the orators on pulpits about cultures – are cultures right or are they wrong? This is a futile debate. When the Prophet came to the world he did not come at the exclusion of cultures and conventions. There was a pre-existing world with its own cultures, languages and morals. He did not create cultures. What he did was he questioned them and shaped them. He questioned them thoroughly. He brought them to a level of fairness. What is Islamic culture, and non-Islamic culture? Every culture is divine, is good, provided it assists in the growth of the individual and the human community. As soon as it begins to bar it, cause it to suffocate and stifle it, that culture needs to be checked as there is nothing sacred about that culture. If it is preventing growth then change it, modify it – we cannot be slaves to the culture that we have created. Is it possible that something we create to make us more Godly is in fact driving us away from God and we are shackled in the name of God. When culture curtails production, we need to question it. For example, all these rituals we have, seriously, if our minds are not focused towards God then are we not doing them in a slavish, formalistic manner as a force of habit? This is not Islam. Why should we be afraid of not following the masses? Do we not use our intellect to think? In 1990, 1980, 1970, the *mehndi* of Hazrat Qāsim would be brought ahead of the *alam*. This was a created culture. If that culture serves a sentiment it's fine, but if it starts to curtail our growth then it needs to be questioned. This is what the Prophet was challenging – the people had created so much false theology and culture that they had lost self-confidence, and that is why there was a straight message from Allah, that the mosque (*masjid*) is *only* for Allah; do not call anybody other than Allah in the *masjid*. Do not adorn the *masjid* to the point of distraction – your focus is only Allah, and Allah is that liberating force. So, religion by priority has to carry that facet of liberating us. This is the reason why the religion was minimalistic. When one refers to culture, it means religious culture and culture otherwise. Every culture is good so long as it produces growth on the basis of the principles that the Quran is supplying – that beautiful Quranic theology of God-centricity. If it curtails growth, then it needs to be challenged.

The Prophet was one head of the whole of the Muslim Ummah. He said, "Me and ʿAlī are the two fathers of this Ummah – not of the Shīʿas. When the Mahdi comes, he will be the father of all *mankind*, leave aside the Ummah." So here is an invitation for us to examine our religion. Is it restrictive? Is it constantly creating divisions between the Muslims and other faiths? If so, then it is totally inconsistent with the Quranic theology. Are its laws based on such principles that they dehumanize the other? Religion is minimalistic. In order to allow scope for growth and evolution, we must examine the theology and practice of religion, the religious culture, and see if they are assisting growth. If they are, then fine, but if they are not assisting growth they need to be challenged. It is also very possible that many of the religious beliefs, its theology, morality and law, can be misinterpretations of people. This is quite possible. These misinterpretations are totally inconsistent with the Godly spirit within us and our intuition. Can Allah command us to that which is reprehensible? Is it possible that such religious beliefs made sense at the time they were issued because of the context in which they were said? For example, some people from our community said that Sayyid Muḥsin al-Ḥakīm had issued a *fatwa*, a legal verdict, that a Sayyid woman cannot get married to a non-Sayyid man in Pakistan because it was leading to bloodshed – so it was only in the context of Pakistan. It did not mean that one person was superior to another person – nor is this (superiority) mentioned anywhere in the Quran. If there was a superiority of one community or lineage, the people would have said to the blessed Prophet that he was not replacing the pagan system at all since the pagans asserted that they were born more privileged and more superior to others. In fact, the Quran states in Surah al-Ḥujurāt, "O men! Behold, We have created you all out of a male and a female, and have made you into nations and tribes, so that you might come to know one another. Verily, the noblest of you in the sight of God is the one who is most deeply conscious of Him. Behold, God is all-knowing, all-aware." (49:13) This is being said to humanity at large.

Night Nine

We stated that Islam is minimalistic – and we want to understand this further as there is a serious misunderstanding about the nature of Islam. Islam is perceived as a system of do's and don'ts. The laws of Islam and the spirituality of Islam are perceived as ceremonies that are performed within the context of Islam and the Muslim community. This brings to mind a notion that Islam is a complete way of life and a complete religion. It has a certain flexibility, but by and large it is very rigid and brings about uniformity. All these things are accurate about Islam. All I want is for us to deliberate on what these things really mean.

By and large, when we talk in a language, the truth is we don't understand what we are talking about. When we examine the words that we are uttering, we see that we don't really understand what they mean. We are assuming their meanings and nobody knows what they are talking about, and nobody is really understanding accurately. For example, the statement, "Allah is just." Without understanding the meaning of Allah, without understanding the meaning of justice, and without understanding the predication, "Allah is just" – how can we say, "Allah is just? Allah is the author of justice. Whatever Allah does in the ambit of existence manifests itself in a balanced state. This brings to mind the notion of justice. Therefore, how can we apply this notion of justice upon the author of justice Himself? For if He were to do things differently, *that would constitute justice as well.* This proves the point that the majority of the time the language we are speaking is something we do not really comprehend. The religion in which we are born and in which we open our eyes is a fully packaged religion. We live it – and before you know it we begin to condemn on its basis, condone on its basis, kill on its basis, and give life on its basis without first asking what does it mean in itself. Am I truly understanding it? The Muslim mind claims that Islam is complete and we need to find answers from within Islam. This claim needs to be examined.

Let us consider this phrase from the third verse of Sūrah al-Māʾida: "This day I have completed for you your religion." (5:3) This verse was revealed at Ghadīr Khum and is understood as, "Today I have completed your religion," which leads to the understanding that there is nothing within the human community, in its societal or individual context, but that it has been responded to by Islam. So there is no more enquiry left. Everything is there. We just have to search it out. However, when this verse was revealed at Ghadīr Khum, the assumption is that every law of Islam was delivered at that point. But history and exegetical literature show that even after Ghadīr Khum the laws of Islam were still being revealed to the blessed Prophet. Since the laws of Islam were still being delivered after this statement, i.e. "I have completed your *dīn*," then what does this verse mean? It definitely does not refer to the law system of Islam. So, this proves that we have not understood the verse correctly.

From 6,200 odd verses of the Holy Quran only 500 pertain to the laws of Islam. The majority are explaining theology and morality through various stories and anecdotes. The whole purpose was that human beings acquire human morals and begin their journey towards Allah. The theology is to become God-like and morality is the attitude and all the beautiful qualities that we ought to acquire. The law system is designed to bring about that beautiful morality. So when this verse says that "Islam is complete," it does not mean that the law of Islam is complete. It can't be since the human community is flowing, evolving, growing: there are different relations being formed at all points and there are different questions that arise at all points. This verse was not referring to the completion of the law system, but was referring to the appointment of Imam ʿAlī ibn Abī Ṭālib – that the Holy Prophet was appointing an authority who would interpret Islam in accordance with the demands of the context, keeping in mind God-centricity and befitting human morality as necessitated by the fluctuating context of the time.

The law system is minimalistic within Islam. The salient principles of Islam are encapsulated in the moral principles, in its theology, which is that we all become God-centric; to become God-like. The religion of Islam is structured in such a way that Allah allows us to discern right from wrong with our minds. He empowers us, and through this process of empowering us, we grow and liberate ourselves. The mistakes we make along the course of growth are a necessary feature of growth and our inbuilt nature; it cannot be otherwise. Judaism was replaced by Christianity and Christianity was replaced by Islam, but Judaism was not replaced by Christianity in the aspect that there is no God-centricity. It actually reasserted and emphasised that there is God-centricity that has been lost within Judaism. Islam did not replace Christianity in the sense of that salient feature of God-centricity and human morality. It replaced Christianity in terms of how to attain that God-centricity which the Christians had altered or the God-centricity that had been forgotten within Christianity, for example, through certain ideas of trinity.

In this way, a religion has to be minimalistic in its law system because these are the things that formulate morality for us. Look at the leverage the Quran gives within its law system. As a punishment and deterrent, we are told that the male and female thief should have their hands cut off. A thief was brought before the second Caliph ʿUmar, who ordered his left hand be cut. He stole again so the right foot was cut. The third time he stole the Caliph ordered his right hand be cut. Imam ʿAlī stopped him and said, "Do not do this as this man will be unable to lead a life; throw him in the prison instead." Imam ʿAlī said, "I will be embarrassed before Allah if I should cut both his hands off and deprive him of all means." Imam ʿAlī pardoned the *sahm al-Imam*. Imam Bāqir issued a statement that, "I pardon the *sahm al-Imam* as my grandfather ʿAlī had done, but I am imposing *khums* on gold and silver." When they cried out, he said that, "It is only for a year because the needs of the community are such that I have to generate revenue to fulfil the needs of the growing community." They were moving the law all the time *according to the needs of the time* in accordance with the salient feature of growth. Quran says, "Establish the prayer and the *zakāt*," without stipulating the amount to be given; nor does it talk about barley, sheep-goats or dates. *Zakāt* is a requirement of a functional community. How else would he make a welfare system, develop the infrastructure and defend his state without taxes? So, the amount is not stipulated as these amounts will have to be determined according to the needs of the time, which are different from era to era and will out of necessity fluctuate.

The completion of Islam is not by this watertight rigid law system, but the completion of Islam is by the designation of a competent authority who could understand how the law is formulated according to the salient principles of growth, God-centricity and the attainment of befitting morals by an individual and the community. Our nature is one of growth and evolution. God-centricity means to direct ourselves to Allah, to be liberated fully and to grow fully. Islam is very mindful of the individual that Allah has created. This individual lives in an individual capacity and a collective capacity – has many facets to their personality. The growth of this individual should be catered for within the individual's context and the society at large. All these have to be supplied by Islam. Islam gives principles for how an individual and society ought to be, but does not give you a social system. It merely outlines the principles of fair-play and of Godliness. This is the right of the individual within the community, and this is the right of the community in context of the individual. There is no such thing as an "Islamic" social system or "Islamic" economy or "Islamic" politics. The Prophet came to a given society which had its language, culture and its ways of doing things. The Prophet tweaked them, modified them, so that they became productive and God-centric. For example, *zakāt* is a societal need. We cannot avoid it whether in the West or in the East. However, in line with God-centricity, Islam adds the element of spirituality within *zakāt*. As Imam ʿAlī states in Nahj al-Balāgha, when you give *zakāt* give with the intention of seeking nearness to God. Bring the Godliness into this mundane act.

If Islam had brought about any morals or principles which were inconsistent with human nature and growth, it would have lost its force with the passage of time. The prophetic Islam is wholesome. It caters for different facets of the human personality yet at the same time it is minimalistic. Today the Muslims are fighting over symbolism in Islam. We find one group of Muslims who denounce symbolism – don't pray *Fatiḥa* at the graves; don't touch the *alams*, etc. Another group sees nothing but symbols. Both are right and both are wrong. They are wrong in being exclusive and they are right in seeing that it's a need of human existence. When a child is in nursery you teach the child through imagery, playdough and clay. So at the level of our humanity, we need symbolism. Islam is a beautiful religion: minimalistic yet wholesome. It is an ongoing process. A religion that does not empower is not from Allah. Allah has not created this brain to be left dormant. That is why we must understand the worth of justice, of coexistence, of harmony, of evolution for our Twelfth Imam to appear. The Holy Prophet left behind his noble progeny, most amazing role models for humanity; but we have not understood them. The role models of Islam are role models for the whole human family and cannot, therefore, leave behind a system that stifles humanity.

At the level of humanity, do we want to grow and harmoniously coexist with the other, appreciate the good in the other, be good to others? Do we want to assert that a person who is sincere is the one who is most Godly regardless of their faith? Do we really assume our Allah to be so petty minded? What are we instilling in the minds of our children? Is it any wonder that we are not producing philosophers and thinkers? This platform of religious sittings (*majālis*) thanks to Imam Ḥusayn should be used for the transformation of the Ummah and empowering reformation if the true Islam was preached – not that of whether it is correct to pray with folded arms or open arms. The Sunnī is cursing the Shīʿa. The Shīʿa is cursing the Sunnī, and if not him then the Brelvī, the Mālikī, the Ṣūfī, the Salafī – all at each other's necks. These are not different readings of the same truth, but rather exclusivist representations of Islam, each one claiming to be the only true Muslim sect heading towards heaven. "Say to the people of the Book, come and let us unite on what is common between us," (3:64) says the Quran.

History needs to be scrutinized to see what is accurate and what is not. We all have to open our minds, study the texts. Who can deny that historically the first Caliph of Islam was Abū Bakr, the Second ʿUmar, the third ʿUthmān, and the fourth ʿAlī ibn Abī Ṭālib? Who can deny that ʿAlī ibn Abī Ṭālib was the most eligible and qualified individual and the rightful successor to the Holy Prophet? Both parties cannot deny, but both parties are stuck to their point of view and are fighting and cursing each other. If Imam ʿAlī or any of the Imams were here today, would they tolerate this disunity in their name? They would say, "Accept what happened in history and move on.... Grow. Become productive."

Night Ten

We have been discussing the theme "Islam, God-Centricity and Human Liberation" and we have made certain fundamental points: that the whole purpose of life is one of growth, of acquiring the fullness of our humanity. The potential is already within us. God-centricity becomes that direction which removes us from all distractions. Islam becomes the vehicle, the means by which we can remove all the distractions and which allows us full growth. Allah empowers us at every point in this journey to reach out to Him. In our human condition we know no restrictions, no boundaries. The boundaries that come upon us are self-imposed. Inevitably, Islam asks for the removal of those limitations, boundaries and barriers. Allah talks of this as "association with God". Allah states, "Allah may forgive every sin for whomever he wishes, but He will not forgive shirk." We ask, why will He not forgive *shirk*? Is it because Allah has a human condition like ours that says, "I don't like this"? I ask "Why?" and He says, "Do not ask Me something I do not like?" Does God have a human condition or is there a profound truth to it? When examined closely we find that it is not He who does not want to forgive *shirk*. *Shirk* is a condition that cannot be forgiven. We cannot force knowledge into the mind and the head of a student until and unless the student becomes receptive to knowledge. Therefore, it is as if God is saying, "Ignorance cannot be exchanged with knowledge because ignorance is an attitude of arrogance; that what I know is best. Ignorance is not the lack of knowledge; it is an attitude that what I have is enough."

So, Allah through God-centricity says, "Give yourself to your natural existential human condition. When you do that you will quickly begin to evolve." Allah gestures at this within the Quran. All names are in your chest, they wish to reveal themselves. That is why Adam was made a point for the prostration of the angels, not because of anything but the nobility of Adam's ability to see beyond himself, which the angels could not understand. Allah therefore constructs a religion. It is one religion (*dīn*) for all of mankind and that is why Allah keeps it singular within the Quran. It has always been one religion; Allah calls this religion "the religion of surrender to the will of Allah." This religion is in sync with the human condition of growth and self-liberation. This religion over the ages has taken on different expressions: Judaism, Christianity, Islam, of those that the people of the Book subscribe to and admit to. In this religion the salient principle, the essential feature, has been God-centricity, self-liberation, self-actualization, individual and communities, flowing to the completion of their full potential. Allah says, "If you wish to penetrate within the depths of the heavens, then do so." When the Sun was being worshipped, Allah said, "I have made it subservient to you." When the seas produced their majestic waves and the human beings felt overawed, Allah said, "I have created the ark for you, and I have made the ocean subservient to you. Go set assail, it is all yours." He empowered the minds and the hearts constantly challenging us to break every boundary, every limit, to arrive at that height destined for us. In addition, in our eschatology, at the end when the Mahdi comes, his fundamental role will not be to teach you how to pray, give *zakāt* or do Hajj. His principle function will be to drive your intellects to their completion. The society of the Mahdi is described as one where people of different faiths will coexist harmoniously. The Islam we described in this process is simplistic and minimalistic. By simplistic what do we mean? It is a religion whose values are immediately understood. You do not need to construct in-depth philosophical arguments, they are very simple. It is minimalistic. It does not have too many laws or regulations. It has at the centre of it the whole theme of becoming Godly, Godlike. Acquire the beautiful morals that befit humanity, and the law-system is a means for you to acquire all of that. This is what Islam is all about, whether it has come in the form of Judaism, Christianity or the formalistic form of "Islam" that we have. The Prophet came to a community that already had its cultures, its language, its ways of doing things, its rights and its wrong. The Prophet spoke their language, carried their sentiment, he appreciated the good of the community, he sympathized with them, he loved them extremely. These were the people who buried their daughters.

If I can share a story with you. A man came to the Prophet intending to accept Islam not knowing whether forgiveness was available for him. He said to the Prophet, "I have buried six daughters. When Allah granted me the seventh one, my wife hid her from me. She said to me, 'It was a stillbirth.' She gave my daughter instead to the neighbours. The neighbours began to raise my daughter, but would send her to us, and because she was the neighbour's daughter I instinctively did not feel the urge of hatred towards her, and instead compassion prevailed my heart and began to shower her with love and affection. When she reached the age of seven, my wife, seeing the affection and kindness I felt towards this young girl, finally confessed to me that it was my daughter, and out of fear of me killing her told me that she had not disclosed the truth to me. O Prophet, I said to this child, 'I will take you to the desert and play a game with you.' I took her to the desert. I said to the child, 'Dig a hole in the sand with me.' She dug a hole with me knowing not why she is digging that hole. I asked her to get into the hole. O Prophet, I began to cover the hole. When it reached her neck, she cried, 'O father, I no longer find this game pleasurable.' Confused and bewildered, this little child, not knowing what is happening, looked at me as I continued to cover the hole until it reached her head and she died." Tears poured from his blessed eyes, and at that moment the Prophet said, "Allah has forgiven you." When the Prophet came he appreciated the practices of the people. He appreciated the good that was there. He questioned the evil that was there. He appreciated the good that was there, made it God-centric, and allowed them to evolve from monsters that buried seven daughters to angels that God praises in the Quran.

He challenged their minds, and the more the opposition grew towards the Prophet, the greater was the force of revelation. The more they mounted their attack, the Quran did not relent – it acquired greater force. It broke their intellectual idols. The whole of the system was tweaked. God that was not there was introduced. And as soon God was introduced, everything became meaningful. Imagine, from people with such superstitions that they would have to make an offering to their God, to people who defied every false god. From people who were unlettered, to people who are the greatest writers of the time. From people who did not know what lay beyond the sands of Arabia, to people who are exploring the world. From people without education, to people who contribute to the knowledge-base of the world. From people who were killing each other in the name of God, to people who were uniting with one another in the name of God. All of this was brought about by the Prophet tweaking the system and changing the essential facet of it. He introduced Allah at the helm of their existence. In your individual life, it is Allah who is the focus. In your communal life, it is Allah who is your focus. Anything that obstructs your growth needs to be challenged, needs to be changed. There is no sacredness in this. So what if your fathers have done this for thousands of years? If it doesn't make sense, it does not make sense. So what if the most learned scholar has said this to you, does it make sense? He said to the Christians, "Even if your argument is that ʿĪsā was born without a father, does that make God his father? Does it make sense? If so, then Adam should be a greater son of God than ʿĪsā. He had no father or mother." If we can revert to the Islam of the Prophet, bring back that centricity of God, everything that is done acquires proper meaning. Everything becomes productive. It gives us growth. 1.7 billion Muslims will become the explorers of this world as they were initially. 1.7 billion Muslims of this world would be contributing to a stable and fair economy. Their minds with the input of the Quran would bring about the best society. They would be greatest humanitarians. Can you imagine?

I will say this, in the 1980s (when I was a child) I would go at night to listen to the religious speaker's talk after the fast and the customary recitations of the Quran was over. He would say, "When the Mahdi comes you will see each other in the palms of your hands." The Muslim in me would say "*Subḥān Allah*! What a miracle the Mahdi will bring!" This text has been with us for you know how long? A thousand years. For a thousand years, the superstitious mind of a Muslim attributes a beautiful technology with miraculous properties and says, "It would be a miracle that the Twelfth Imam would bring." No confidence in my own humanity. And then when the non-Muslim brings about mobile technology and we begin to see each other in the palm of our hands, we say, "*Subḥān Allah*! We had this text from one thousand years ago!" I will say, "Shouldn't you be beating your heads in embarrassment and regret instead? Shouldn't you be crying that you are the greatest failure. You did not know how to read your text for a thousand years?" If the non-believer who we say is a non-believer had seen this text, mobile technology would have emerged five hundred years ago. Do you realise this? Because they would know that something like this is possible instead of accidently coming across it.

It is strange that the Muslim takes pride that he had such futuristic texts. To be honest with you, if this feat of technology has been achieved, then the person who stumbled across it is a greater believer of Mahdi than I am because he is bringing closer the era of Mahdi – as opposed to somebody like me who reads it as miraculous traditions (*ḥadīth*). It questions my notion of disbeliever (*kāfir*) and Muslim altogether. This is something that we have been trying to question; has that God-centricity left Islam? Have we, as the

Muslim Ummah, reverted to the sentiments of the pagans within the fold of Islam? Is it the same story now that was prevalent prior to the Prophet in the form of Lāt and ʿUzza? Is the same story prevalent today in the name of God Himself? Is it the same sentiment that pollutes the beautiful Islamic values?

It is a grand night. I want to ask a certain question here; we need to be honest with ourselves. You see the community is a genuine community, a gem of a community. I'll explain why – this is a community which, after abandoning its homes in Africa, did not care about its own houses but creates the house of God and the house of the Prophet first. This is how loyal the community is. It is a community which, if given the truth, will evolve and swiftly arrive at the summits of mankind, contribute to it meaningfully and lead the way as Imam Jaʿfar al-Ṣādiq has said in relation to the definition of a Shīʿa. It is a beautiful community, lovely community. If the truth is given to it, it will flourish. It will break all boundaries, and I know it will accept the truth given to it. Tell me – and I ask this often – had me and you not been Muslims, would we choose Islam as our faith? And if we chose Islam as our faith, which Islam would we choose? Sunnism? Shīʿism? Salafism? Deobandi Islam? Sufism? Ismailism? Twelver Shīʿism? Which one? Which one would we choose as our faith? And if we chose any of one of them as our faith, would we subscribe to the whole lock, stock and barrel of it or would we have reservations? If we were objective, how much of this Islam would we choose?

There was a group of women that came to me. They said, "There is this hadith that says the women are weak in their faith and intellect. I believe in it but only in a specific context. Imam ʿAlī has said this but it is in a befitting context." I said to these women, "Do you actually believe this, do you believe in this statement?" They said, "It is from Imam ʿAlī." I said, "But does it make sense?" They said, "No." This is what I ask. If somebody says that *ḥadīth*, then a woman has the God-given right to say that he himself had the queen of women as his wife. He, whilst he lived, never said "no" to Fāṭima. He says, "Take advice from women and do its opposite!" You've heard this right? Seek advice from women and do its opposite so she dare not speak in front of you again. But history records that so long as Lady Fāṭima was alive, Imam ʿAlī is seen as a defiant man, full of strength. As soon as she dies, he becomes docile, takes himself to the house and locks himself up. Lady Fāṭima was his pillar of strength. Look at Lady Zaynab, she does something Imam al-Sajjād could never have done – and I say this and I know it is the truth. Do you know, when Yazīd was poking at the face of Ḥusayn ibn ʿAlī in front of the captives, you find that Imam al-Sajjād was unable to lift his head due to the grief he was suffering. Then suddenly, this woman, Lady Zaynab, stands and unleashes words that are sharper than a thousand blades. "Son of freed slaves!" she says to him. Do you know how eloquently she constructs her sermon (*khuṭba*) in which the verses of the Quran, the historical facts, the state of Karbala, the mind-set of Yazīd and all around her are brought together? How can a person compose such an eloquent sermon like this extemporaneously? It has to be a highly-qualified mind that can do this. Imam al-Sajjād could never have performed that task, he could never have done it. Zaynab was the only one who could have performed that task. It's a given. We all know this. How beautifully and eloquently she puts him in his place. Do you know what she says? She says, and this is extemporaneously, "It is befitting of somebody like you, O Yazīd..." because Yazīd exclaimed, "If only my ancestors at Badr were present today, they would condone me and say, 'Yazīd, well done! You have sought revenge for the events at Badr.'" She says, "It befits the likes of you, whose meat and bones have been strengthened by women's milk which has been formed through chewing livers of the friends of God." Imagine the way she puts it together, is it not amazing? "It befits the likes of you, whose meat and bones have been strengthened by women's milk which has been formed through chewing livers of the friends of God!" She says, "If only you could hear your forefathers, they would be crying out to you saying, 'Silence, Yazīd, Silence! For we know the wrong that we did.'" She says, "It befits the likes of you who cut the heads of the friends of Allah and tear their bodies apart, and the hyenas walk all over them leaving their imprints on their chests." The eloquence with which she speaks. ʿAlī ibn Abī Ṭālib had Fāṭima as his wife whom he always listened to. So, ask these women, "Does it make sense to you? If it does not, then ask somebody to justify it. If it can't be justified then question it further."

So, again I ask this question, if you and I had not taken birth in Islam would we choose Islam as a religion? If so, which branch of Islam? If so, would it be the whole lock, stock and barrel or would we be averse to certain facets of this Islam? With full confidence, anybody studying the history of the Prophet of Islam, ʿAlī ibn Abī Ṭālib, Ḥasan, Ḥusayn, Ṣādiq, till the Eleventh Imam will not accept an Islam that is divisive. I say this with full confidence because it is inconsistent with their teaching. It is inconsistent with our human condition. So here it is, what really happens is that *we have the truth within ourselves*. We have discussed this, but I want to talk about it again so there is no mind amongst us with any ambiguity – and please forgive me if at times my words have been blunt, hurtful or sharp – forgive me. I am a humble servant of yours and a slave of Allah, and if I say anything wrong please point it out so that you can guide me aright. So here is what I said in one of the lectures: "the truth is within us, we project it outside." So now, we stated that when a Hindu respects and venerates Rām, he does so because he sees all the beautiful Godly qualities in Rām. He says, "Rām is brave, he is truthful, he is charitable, he is eloquent, he is altruistic." All the beautiful qualities of humanity and Godliness he sees in the face of Rām, and that is why he respects Rām. If you look at the follower of Buddha, he will find the same beautiful qualities in the face of Buddha. If you look at the follower of Mūsā he will do the same, ʿĪsā – same, the Prophet of Islam – same, ʿAlī ibn Abī Ṭālib – same, first Caliph, Abū Bakr – same, second Caliph, ʿUmar – same, third Caliph, ʿUthmān – same. Nobody respects Rām because Rām was a liar, or because he was a cheat, or because he was a coward, or because he swore at this mother. They respect Rām for the positive beauty that he had. Can you see that? In that way, what happens is that we are all venerating the same truth, but we give this truth different faces. The truth is in us: those faces for us exemplify the truth. That truth which is inside us, when we project it outside us, naïvely whatever face carries that truth we wholeheartedly accept that entity in its entirety without any question. Can you see that? I am coming to the point – we see the beautiful Godly truth in Islam.

The Prophet is other than this formal Islam. Imam ʿAlī is other than this formal Islam. I need to make this distinction first. When we subscribe to the Prophet in the entirety, the Prophet is splendid in his entirety. ʿAlī ibn Abī Ṭālib is splendid in his entirety. But when we see the truth in Islam we naïvely subscribe to the whole of the religion, and then we don't question much of it that does not make any sense. Not only do we not question it, we end up justifying it. Can you see that? Look within ourselves: if we find any facet negative, so long as it comes with the label of Islam, what would be our reaction? Not to question, but to justify it. Fine, Islam is a glorious religion, but the Islam that me and you have got today is the product of 1,400 years of history. How much of it is true Islam? How much of it is the formulation of ordinary people in accordance with their own understanding? Can you see that? How much of it is Islam of the Prophet? How much of it is formulation? By "formulation," what I mean is those beautiful values were given shape and form, and then practiced by the people of the past. How much of it is practice of the people of the past, how much of it is the Islam of the Prophet? You see the hadith says that when the Mahdi comes they will point at him and say, "He changes our religion, this is not our religion." So, what is our religion? I ask those people who point the finger at Mahdi and say, "this is not our religion" – so what is our religion? If he is the grandson of the Prophet and the crowning glory of Islam then what he is bringing cannot be alien to what the Prophet had brought. Just as the Prophet had said, "I have brought what Mūsā and ʿĪsā brought." He said to the Jews, "I believe in everything that has been revealed to me, and I believe in everything revealed to you, because it is the same thing. So whatever I am saying to you is not alien to what Moses and ʿĪsā said. Whatever you, O people, have brought about in the name of religion, it is alien to the teachings of ʿĪsā and Mūsā."

So, when the Mahdi comes and the people point fingers at him and say, "This is not the religion of Muḥammad," then I will say, "Who knows better the religion of Muḥammad than the Mahdi?" Obviously, when you think about it you begin to understand very quickly that the religion will be so much adulterated, so much moved away from God-centricity, simplicity and minimalism, that when the Mahdi comes with the religion of the Prophet, it won't be recognisable. Can you see that? How amazing is this? As we pointed out yesterday, when the Mahdi comes he will be acknowledged by Christians and Jews alike. But the naïve Muslim thinks that the Mahdi will make everybody pray with their arms open. He is not like that at all. He is the *crème de la crème* of humanity. His concerns are other concerns, greater concerns, Godly concerns, lofty concerns, to create a state that is conducive for human growth. The man is lofty; we have reduced him to a very low level of sectarianism.

A lot of people have asked me to clarify certain themes today which we will do. So those themes were charity (*ṣadaqa*). They have asked me, "What do you mean 'Don't give *ṣadaqa*?'" I never said, "Don't give *ṣadaqa*." I said, "Praise be to God! (*al-ḥamdu li-Llāh*). May God create more black cats so we give more *ṣadaqa*." That is what I said. But let us explain with an example as to what we meant and how we have misunderstood things. Everything is geared around God-centricity – where things become productive and make sense. The religious texts say, "If you are good to your mother, Allah increases your livelihood. If you are good to your mother, Allah repels all evils from you. If you are good to your mother, Allah gives you a long life." Now there two types of people listening to this. There is one who is good to his mother because she is his mother, everything else is a bonus on the side. Can you see that? I am good to my mother because I owe her my existence.

I am terribly in love with my mother. I would rather God take my life away and give it to my mother. I would rather all calamities befell me and not my mother. Can you see that? Or the text says, "If you are good with your children, Allah gives you a long life. Allah removes calamities." So the person who understands says, "O Allah, take away all calamities from my children and put them on me. Extend the life of my children and give me death quickly. Give them health and give me sickness." That's the attitude, right?

But then you have another person: "O Allah, I'm only going to visit my mother because I want to multiply my one million to two million." That attitude is the wrong attitude. "I am good to my children because Allah can ward off all calamities from me." No! Be good to your children because you are reflected in your children. Be good to your mother because she is your origin. Love her blindly without any want of gain; the gain will come automatically when you're good to her. Can you see that? And that is why the Prophet said, "Removing a stone from the road in order to bring ease to the travellers is *ṣadaqa* in the way of Allah." The attitude is "O Lord, I am doing this so that others may not stumble upon it and fall and break their limbs." That is the attitude of *ṣadaqa*, the God-centric attitude. Give *ṣadaqa* as much as we can but let's not be businessmen in *ṣadaqa*. Yes, once in a while, when we have a court case, we give *ṣadaqa* to say to Allah, "O Allah, through this I invoke your assistance." Once in a while we go to our mothers, we massage her feet and say, 'Pray for me so that I am successful in this or that." Once in a while we contract a business deal, but by and large the attitude is it is something that needs to be done of its own merit without any gain or loss.

We must ask, "What is God-centric means-seeking (*wasīla*)? *Wasīla* is to seek the attention of God, the presence of God, through God Himself and His handiwork. This is what *wasīla* is. If anybody is any doubt about this, read the authentic prayers of our Imams and al-Ṣaḥīfa al-Sajjādiyya. Read it and you will see, "O Lord, I beseech you by your Name 'Allah.' I beseech you through your beautiful Names, '*al-Raḥmān*,' '*al-Raḥīm*.' O Lord, I beseech you through your beautiful handiwork, through the beautiful heavens and the Earth you have created. O Lord, I beseech you through the proximate angels. O Lord, I beseech you though your Prophets. O Lord, I beseech you through the best of your creation, Muḥammad, and the progeny of Muḥammad." What are we doing here? We are making God the centre. The approaches to God are multiple, but through God-centricity. That is what it meant by *wasīla* – proper *wasīla*. There cannot be any facet of Islam that distracts from the unity of God and God-centricity. There cannot be. It is not possible. The Quran, the prophets, and the Imams do not teach us to approach God through anything other than God – that would be *shirk*.

We come to intercession (*shafāʿa*). Allah says in the Quran, "There is no intercession save with the consent of Allah." (2:255) So the centricity again is with God. The statements of the Prophet and the Imams also make this clear. They say, "Look, we cannot do anything save by the decree of God and you yourself being good." So intercession (*shafāʿa*), as Ṭabāṭabāʾī discusses in his *tafsīr*, is to add something to something else to make it dual and strengthen it; to make one thing into two things. Now, the day of *qiyāmah* is a very humanlike understanding. Everything you want to know about the hereafter, you should first understand through the example of this world, and then you will begin to understand the terms of the hereafter. So now, if a person loves Muḥammad, ask yourself, "Why does he love Muḥammad"? For *godliness*. For the beauty that is within Muḥammad. So as soon as they love Muḥammad for his godliness, for the beauty that is within Muḥammad, then the blessed Prophet Muḥammad has acquired an esteemed position within their souls. Their souls are now becoming God-centric. The deficiencies that are within their souls are then compensated through Prophet Muḥammad on the Day of Reckoning. But Prophet Muḥammad can only do that if the soul already recognises Muḥammad. However, if I were to venerate the blessed Prophet Muḥammad without god-centricity then I am not venerating the real person, he is not there.

Prophet Muḥammad is Prophet Muḥammad through his absolute godliness. If I have appreciated the real Messenger of God, then there is godliness in me already. Can you see that? If I have respected the Messenger of God at the exclusion of godliness then that Muḥammad is not to be found anywhere. Like the Quran says, "On the Day of Reckoning, call upon the people you called on in the world, they will call and find no response!" (28:64) Allah says, "They are not there because you never called on the real person." The real person of the Prophet is one who is godly, so if we fall in love with that godly person, then that real person in his godliness is within us and the lack is compensated for because that aptitude is there and that aptitude is then acknowledged and then completed. It is like somebody is inside a prison and the judge says, "Look, this man has committed petty crimes, but if you want to bail him out, you can bail him out. I respect you that much, and if you say to me that he is good enough and you can rectify him then I trust you, you can do it but he is your responsibility." The Prophet has said a man will be raised with whomever he loves – that is the meaning of intercession (*shafāʿa*), not at the exclusion of God but very much with the inclusion of God. If I love this pulpit at the exclusion of God, then it becomes a calamity for me. It will become a point of damnation for me. It must be God-centric, nothing can be at the exclusion of God. If this ring that I am wearing becomes at the exclusion of God, it is *shirk*. Anything done at the exclusion of God is a distraction, and Allah asks us to challenge that.

The history of the Muslims needs to be checked. Me and you are a product of the history fed to us. We have a God-given right to criticize that history and ask pertinent questions such as whether any of it makes any sense. Now, I'll give a mundane example. As a child, I grew up hearing that ʿAbbās killed a thousand people to his right. Then when we grew up somebody says, "How long does it take to kill a thousand people?" Obviously, it is a question that intrigues the mind. I grew up having heard that Imam ʿAlī prayed a thousand units (*rakʿāt*) of prayer every night. Have you ever asked yourselves how long it would take to pray a thousand *rakʿāt*? And then he used to work, fight in battles, was a statesman and so and so forth. How did it all happen? Someone just told me two days ago that the great companion Ḥurr heard the children crying, "We are dying of thirst." Upon hearing this he defected from the camp of Yazīd to the camp of Imam Ḥusayn. Some people have asked, "Why couldn't he have taken water with him if he knew they are thirsty?" Can you see this? These are examples which might seem very humble examples, but they intrigue the mind. Ask questions. Is this history that is being narrated to us accurate? Are the ceremonies we perform distracting? Or are they leading to God? Are they liberating us or not?

I was in Bombay, and where I was staying there was a temple nearby outside the hotel. In the early mornings, the people would gather to carry out their religious ceremonies. It was early and I woke up from all the noise. I looked outside and I said, "Oh, what a beautiful scene!" The same thing happened on the second day, and the third day and the fourth. By the seventh day I got tired of it. I said, "Don't you have anything better to do? You know this constant rattle and noise, we can't even sleep anymore. You worshipped your God once – why do you have to worship Him seven days with the same noise and commotion?" Then I understood that six to eight months each year these people perform such devotional practices. And I said, "But is it something that is good? Such devotion, is it making them into greater humans? Is it making them into greater scientists, or explorers, or people that are contributing to human knowledge? Is it making them into thinkers?" The answer is no. At this point we need to question: are these ceremonies distracting us?

To the best of this humble creature's knowledge, the Prophet and the Imams are *par excellence* role models. They will not leave behind a practice that is detrimental or damaging – and if they have suggested a practice authentically, and if it is detrimental, then in its original context it was productive, and we have to search and find out what that context was. Tell me, we are talking about the sixth Imam, Jaʿfar al-Ṣādiq, the mind of all minds, the *crème de la crème* of all humanity. Do you really think he would contribute anything to the Shīʿa heritage that would result in a bloodbath later? Do you really think he would say, "Allah, curse the first, the second and the third..." and then knowing full well that my followers will recite this and then that this would result in massacres and senseless killings? Does this thing not beg a question? An Imam who was telling people not to disunite, not to allow sectarianism to emerge, not to allow for this strife, to pray with each other, to visit each other, to be good to each other. Do you think that the same Imam would then say something to his followers which they would then practice and in doing so would lead to wholescale bloodshed?

And the greatest enemy of Allah is who? Iblīs. Iblīs is the greatest enemy of Allah. Allah curses Iblīs. How many times a day do I curse Iblīs? Do I hate Iblīs? Obviously, in my day-to-day practices I don't. Why am I not angry at Iblīs? When Imam Ḥusayn came to Imam al-Sajjad, he asked, "What has happened?" The Imam said, "Shayṭān has overpowered their hearts." Why don't they curse Iblīs? Iblīs is the one I am supposed to curse, am I not? The first point of curse should be Iblīs because he's the one misguiding all according to our understanding. Furthermore, the Imam has said, "Iblīs has prevailed upon their hearts." When I curse Iblīs, what am I doing? You know, the meaning of "curse" is not only the removal of mercy from something; it's also the removal of that tendency in me. So when I am getting angry, I say, "O Allah, curse Iblīs!" so the anger can leave *my* heart. When I'm about to lie I say, "O Allah, curse Shayṭān" so that I don't lie. When I am about to steal I say, "O Allah, curse Shayṭān" so I don't steal. So when I say "God's curse be upon Shayṭān," Shayṭān is laughing. He's saying, "You're sending curses upon me but I'm inside you. As the Prophet and Imam ʿAlī have said, "Your Shayṭān is you yourself. Your real Iblīs is you." So sending curses on Iblīs does not mean that you are sending curses on some fanciful creature we have imagined in our heads. The real curse is on that Iblīs inside me, as if I am saying "Allah, remove *me* from this inconsistency."

Isn't that supposed to be the real meaning of cursing? Every act is supposed to be productive. So when we send curses on the enemies of the Family of the Prophet (*ahl al-bayt*), what are we saying? We are saying, "Curse be on every tendency that is ungodly, destructive, regressive, distracting, that takes us away from Allah." Isn't this what cursing is supposed to be? What else can be cursing through God-centricity? Cursing is not personal hatred. Indeed, a God-centric heart cannot hate – hatred is itself a curse. Abusive language and swearing are indicative that one performing these acts is cursed. These are the things we need to be mindful of. We need to bring back ourselves to that beautiful Prophetic Islam: the one that will come with the Mahdi.

Night Eleven

Praise be to Allah through whose grace we witnessed the blessed ten days of Muharram, and through which we refreshed our faith (*īmān*). Over these blessed days of Muharram, we have been discussing the theme of "Islam and God-centricity" to question our outlook towards the world – to discern whether it is a befitting outlook that is allowing us to achieve our life-purpose. We questioned a few things within this. We stated that the world is a place of growth. Hence it is inconceivable that God sent us here not with our consent, but rather through our demand. If God gave us a choice and we came into this world, then God would still be blamed for luring us and enticing us into something that was not worthy. Therefore, this world is the outcome of our demand.

To explain this further: there is a young man in a remote village who wants to educate himself but there are no institutions, instructors, libraries or books in this village. So a very benevolent person sees the yearning of this young man and realises that this man cannot educate himself anywhere else since he is unable to travel outside the village. The benevolent person also realises that the young man can only be educated through a gradual process, so he goes out of his way to create institutions, libraries and instructors. After everything is completed, he sends the student to the establishment to educate himself. Now, here we can see that this man has done a great favour upon the student, and hence the student needs to be grateful to that man for making his education possible. This is our relationship with Allah. We demanded an opportunity to arrive at the fullness of our potential. Allah had to go out of His way to create everything, and after creating everything for our purpose in our context He created the crowning glory known as this Earth. Do you not to see the stellar system beyond the skies, the majestically burning stars and endless galaxies? He has created softness, texture, colour schemes, sense perception, and emotions. This is an outcome of billions and billions of years of work before we could come to this world. We are indebted to Him for all that He has done for us, and hence we thank Him. For example, if a parent continuously demands a child to thank him or her for bringing the child into this world, the child would question why she should thank the parent when this world is rife with challenges and difficulties, where millions are dying, where there is so much hatred and poverty. The child may even accuse the parents for their selfishness in bringing her into this world simply because they wanted to share something between them. Why should the child thank the mother for staying awake at night, feeding and clothing the child, when this was the only way the child could be reared? This is a legitimate question. We must realise that our parents have been passages and means for us to come into this world because we chose them. In fact we have to thank them for all that they have sacrificed for us. This is the type of perception we need to acquire. God is the bestower and you cannot bestow upon someone without their request. If He has created me in need of oxygen, then it is His duty to provide oxygen; it's not a bestowal. I need gravity. I need rain.

This brings us to the definition of success. In the example of the young man who wanted to be educated, what is success for this student? Success was not assessed by how many books he amassed or how many classes he attended. The true success for the student is that he *grows* through the knowledge. So the success of the student is within the student himself. Success of the student is in his ability to actualise the knowledge by passing the exams and getting the qualification for the line of study that he has chosen. What is success for you and me? "I" am not my body because when I am laid to rest in my grave, my body will disintegrate. Even my brain will deteriorate over time. So what is this "I"? I am my success and failure. I am the paradise and I am the hell. I create my inferno and I create my gardens.

The other issue we discussed was "worldview" – what worldview can sustain our growth? The answer we gave is that the true worldview is the one that drives home the meaning that *you* are the point of success and the point of failure. Now, you and I are in a context that is limited and restricted. If the worldview is accurate, then this worldview would determine that this restriction must break to grow like the seed which needs to break itself so that the young plant can begin to sprout from within the Earth. If our worldview is accurate, we will know that everything is geared towards our growth – morally, intellectually and spiritually. When I die, at whatever age, a spiritual individual has already taken birth. To explain this further, when I am twenty I may be praying to God with the impression in my mind that he will help me pass my exams. At twenty-five my thoughts might be focused on my sustenance. At thirty-five I may be praying for my children. At the age of forty my mind is totally different, as then I realise that everything I have been worrying about has been taken care of in order for me to reach this age. At the age of fifty my heart opens up. At 60, when I say, "Dear Lord, Dear Lord," the throne of Allah begins to tremble with the intensity of my supplication. That is when the spiritual person is taking birth – the real person is taking birth and yearning the hereafter, the new birth, the new mother, the new lap, the new beginning, the origin that is the end. The love of my heart re-enters my heart afresh; the light of all lights that I forgot in my youth, I now re-attain. If this is my outlook then it is here where Allah becomes the point of focus and centrality. "O you who yearns everything, it is I that you yearn. If you want unending life, then I am the unending life. If you yearn wealth that has no poverty, I am the wealth unending. If you yearn strength in which there is no weakness, I am the strength. If you yearn control where this is no lack, I am the control. If you yearn knowledge in which there is no ignorance, then I am that." So then there is that invitation from the core, "Yearn Me, and you will acquire your own self." To achieve this Allah puts a mechanism in place. That mechanism is a process of surrender to Allah. That surrender is full yet minimalistic in form. It has to be empowering, for I have to take decisions with confidence. You are not an individual who has been created to live in the comfort of the house. You are an explorer, a voyager; set sail and go forward. Do not look at the sky and wonder. Stretch your hand and grab every star you want. Do not stand at the shores of the ocean wondering what is in it, dive into it.

Islam has to be minimalistic. When it comes to communal practices, Islam has to be minimalistic. Do not read lengthy prayers in a ritualistic fashion without thinking. Let the individuals in their lonely hours attend to the night prayers. Why are night prayers so important? Because obligatory (*wājib*) prayers are done in order to maintain the identity of the Ummah, whereas night prayers are performed for the love of Allah. It's a loyal slave who will sacrifice his sleep for Allah. Allah says, "Devote yourself in loneliness to Me individually, because *you* are the thing that I want." We need to check all our ceremonies against this. Why does the Twelver Shīʿa Muslim point fingers at the Sunnī Muslim for praying additional prayers (*al-nawāfil*) and for institutionalizing them as a congregational practice of *tarāwīḥ*? Was not the Prophet adamant that we pray extra optional prayers in our loneliness? When these people are cursing those people for introducing a practice in the congregational capacity, why do they not look at the number of practices they have introduced in congregational capacity? Surely, a man of God has to be on the pedestal of neutrality and have clarity. When Islam is minimalistic, it allows us space to improvise and grow, to benefit through our experiences. Therefore, we are the success and we are the failures. Our worldview is one in which we need to be empowered to arrive at the fullness of ourselves. This is depicted by Allah being at the helm of our existence. The system that we follow is a flexible system that allows for us to become Godly through God-centricity.

Today's Islam has become so formalistic and restrictive that the growth property, the essence of which is Godliness, has diminished. When we look at the exegesis of the verse, "Lord do not make us of those that are you are angered by nor of those who have transgressed" (1:7) – which is a bigger condemnation? Without doubt the one's whom God is angered by is a much bigger condemnation than those who have been led astray. Some people have strayed off the path, but the others are people whom Allah has damned and condemned. Therefore, the condemned are far worse off. In the *tafsīr*, "those upon whom Your anger falls" is described as the Jewish tendency because of their over emphasis on the form, whereas "those who are misguided" is described as the Christian tendency because of their lack of emphasis on the form and their focus on the essence. Allah is not just talking about the Jews and the Christians, but He is referring to tendencies of humanity at large. For example, the Jews, according to the Quran, were told not to fish on the day of the Sabbath. Ironically, it was on the Sabbath when there were the most fish in the river and the sea. This is how they were being tested. To circumvent this, the Jews put their nets in the water on Friday so the fish could be caught and took their nets out of the water on Sunday, all the while thinking they could outwit God. As a result of this God turned them into apes. These people were highly formalistic to the extent that the essence was compromised and totally taken away. On the other hand, the Christian tendency of focusing solely on the essence meant there was no direction for the formulation of the essence. This is something we need to learn from.

We need to revisit the examples of our blessed Prophet and Imams in which they demonstrate the beautiful balance between form and essence. Prayer is not prayer when there is no God in the heart, when we are not properly thinking about what we are doing. Surely the prayer of a person who is trembling through the remembrance of Allah is more pleasing to Allah? Therefore, essence is predominant over the form, and form is minimalistic. Everything should be leading to Godliness empowering us and freeing us of our restrictions. In this way, we need to examine everything that we are doing. If this is understood, that God-centricity and self-liberation is the only task at hand. If these are understood, then every value of Islam, every practice within Islam, needs to be weighed up against it – whether it is individual or communal.

If we look at the theology and the tenets of Islam, there are only three: belief in one God (*tawhid*), belief in the prophets and messengers send by God (*risālah*) and belief in the Day of Reckoning (*qiyāmah*). For salvation, Allah says, "Believe in God and the Day of Reckoning (*qiyāmah*)" – only two. A Muslim is defined by three things: belief in one God (*tawḥīd*), belief in the prophets (*risālah*) and belief in the Day of Reckoning (*qiyāmah*) – only three. So where did justice (*ʿadl*) come from? It came from the historical debate between Muslim theologians, the Asharites and the Mutazilites. The Asharites were understood as saying that God compels us into action, whereas the Mutazilites argued we have free will; otherwise God would not be just. So, another article was introduced alongside the belief in one God: the belief that God is just (*ʿādil*). But justice (*ʿadl*) should have been part and parcel of belief in God (*tawḥīd*) anyway. So you are not adding anything: you are just further explicating the belief in God's unity (*tawḥīd*). Likewise, prophethood (*nubuwwa*) and leadership (*imāma*) sprung from another theological debate. Yet *imāma* is a part of one's loving devotion (*wilāya*) to the prophets, which is expressed through prophethood (*nubuwwa*) and the blessed Prophet of Islam and later in the form of the beautiful Imams. Whatever has been added to the tenets of faith has been merely due to historical debates and reactions. It is not a part of our theology. We need to check our history and theology. Similarly, we have the notions of loving (*tawallī*) the *ahl al-bayt* and hating (*tabarrī*) the enemies of the *ahl al-bayt*. This too has to be God-centric. It cannot be other than through God centricity. So what is loving (*tawallī*)? Authority (*wilāya*) is only of Allah's. Allah says, "Allah is the *walī* of those who believe." Allah is the *walī*. It is only the *wilāya* of Allah that is then extended to the Prophets and the Imams and as a result we adhere to their authority – but the only authority is Allah. Essentially, *wilāya* is only Allah's. So if a person is saying I am doing *tawallī*, then that person has to be most Godly since *tawallī* is yearning to be Godly – this is what it means in essence. If you are truly doing *tawallī*, then it means that at every point you are becoming Godly. Indeed, if I am following the example of the Prophet, then I am being God-centric because there is nothing but Godliness and God-centricity in the example of the blessed Prophet. When have any of the Prophets or Imams displayed any sectarian tendencies through *tawallī*? Their *tawallī* was God-centricity; their *tawallī* made them transcend human limitations. Anyone within the fold of *wilāya* must arrive at a pedestal of godliness so that they go beyond religious limitations. Is Ḥusayn a Muslim? He is a Muslim of the highest stature, the sort of Muslim that attracts the Hindus, the Christians and the Jews alike. In Ḥusayn we find a true Muslim that appeals to humanity at large. Therefore, *tawallī* in essence is not a point of division, but a point of transcendence through godliness. A person who is performing *tawallī* is actually aiming for the highest pedestal destined for mankind.

What is *tabarrī*? What does it mean? *Tabarrī* is not a fundamental. *Tabarrī* is anything inconsistent with *tawallī*. Through *tabarrī* I am burying, acquitting and absolving myself from anything that is ungodly. So, if I say I am doing *tabarrī* from the enemy of the Prophet Muḥammad, then I am doing *tabarrī* from lying, from cheating, from abusive language, from having a hard heart, from not being merciful – this is *tabarrī*. Similarly, when I am sending curses on Shayṭān, I am inadvertently cursing all the negative tendencies in me. Shayṭān is the greatest enemy of God, but is he not a monotheist? Does he not believe in Allah? Shayṭān says on the Day of Reckoning, "We all did what now transpires as the fires of hell, we all deserve this fate. I am not going to shout and cry about it, so don't shout and cry at me. Be dignified about it. We chose this fate, so let us burn with dignity." Even Shayṭān is dignified.

He believes in *tawḥīd*. He believes in Allah and His attributes. He believes in the Day of Reckoning (*qiyāmah*). He believes in all the Muslim tenets. Yet he is the biggest enemy of Allah – that is the truth that is within us. So when we are doing *tawallī* it means we are being Godly. When we are doing *tabarrī* it means that we are pulling out of our chests anything that is inconsistent with that godliness. As Rumi says, "O person look within your own soul, you will see so clearly that the Ḥusayn within is being butchered by your own Shimr and Yazīd. The one whom you are cursing outside is being nurtured within you."

Someone asked about saying "O ʿAlī, help us" (*yā ʿAlī madad*). If the sons of ʿAlī have said "O ʿAlī, help us!" then we will say it because they teach us the best practice. You will not find any prayer or supplication (*dūʿa*) in which Imam Ṣādiq has said, "O ʿAlī, help us!" Any action that is not in accordance with our faith is a distraction. If the Imam had considered reciting this as best practice, he would have said it. If my faith hinges on pronouncing something, then I will tell you a hadith of Imam Ṣādiq and the blessed ʿĪsā. Prophet ʿĪsā was asked how it felt to be a spirit of God, to be able to resurrect the dead, cure the leper, give sight to the blind, walk on water. He replied that being a humble member of the Ummah of Muḥammad would have meant more to him than being a Messiah and ʿĪsā, the Spirit of Allah. Imam Ṣādiq was asked how it felt to be such a great giant of knowledge. He replied that being a humble follower of ʿAlī ibn Abī Ṭālib meant more to him than being the Sixth Imam. Therefore, even if it is theologically accurate and valid, if the Imam has not committed himself to these things then should we not be questioning any action that is distracting from God-centricity? Should we not be emulating what the Imam did instead? In everything we do, we need to examine our actions and look at the best practices of the role models whom Allah has ordained. We should be working towards arriving at the beautiful state of God-centricity where Allah is pleased. His Prophet and Imam ʿAlī look forward to receiving us on the Last Day. The Mahdi awaits to come to us where everything is geared towards Allah.

God centricity culminates in a vision of Allah – when that point arrives nothing else matters. Imam Ḥusayn, our master, says, "O Allah! Now I have understood that everything in this world, all your creation, every relation, was just there for you to introduce Yourself to me, when my mother glanced affectionately at me it was You looking through her eyes; it was my father who supported me unrestrictedly but it was You Who was providing for me through him; it was my brother who was my pillar of strength but it was You Who was revealing your support through my brother; it was a friend who accepted me unconditionally but it was You Who was introducing Yourself through a friend – O Lord, it was none but You. O Lord, when were You far that I needed to come close to You? You were always near! It was I who has remained at a distance from You. O Lord, when were You hidden that I needed to see You? Blind are the eyes who cannot see You watching over us!" And then the Imam comes to that epic line, "O Lord, what has he lost the one who has found You; and what has he found the one who has lost You?" How beautifully he arrives at the pedestal of Godliness. Similarly, Imam ʿAlī expresses his sentiments for Allah in the famous supplication known as Duʿā al-Kumayl:

> *O my Lord! By Thy honour truly do I swear that, if Thou wilt allow my power of speech to be retained by me in the hell, I shall amongst its inmates cry out bewailingly unto Thee like the cry of those who have faith in Thy kindness and compassion. And I shall bemoan for Thee (for being deprived of nearness to Thee) the lamentation of those who are bereaved, and I shall keep on calling unto Thee: "Where art Thou o' Friend of the believers! O' (Thou who art) the last hope and resort of those who acknowledge Thee and have faith in Thy clemency and kindness; o' Thou who art the helper of those seeking help! O' Thou who art dear to the hearts of those who truly believe in Thee! And o' Thou who art the Lord of the universe.*

The way he says it is so beautiful: "O Lord, if You were to turn a deaf ear to me, a blind eye, it will hurt me to no extent. I don't care what the rest of the world does – I have invested my love in You; for You to ignore me there is no pain greater than that." This is ʿAlī – he expresses the kind of love that is unknown. To understand this let's take the analogy of a mother who loves a child dearly, and the child says, "O mother, look at me, don't ignore me – shout at me, slap me, but don't be oblivious of me as I cannot bear your indifference." Imam ʿAlī opens his heart to Allah. Feel the intimacy of Imam ʿAlī with Allah as he says, "O Lord, how can I bear the pain of Your indifference to me?" Our Fourth Imam says, "O Allah, if You were to cast me into the flames of hell and if that was the only path leading to You, I would surely embrace the fire and call out to the tormentors in hell that I burn in the love of the one who burns me." This is the meaning of God-centricity – the utmost state of liberation. Have you ever known of a father whose young son has a dagger in his chest and he does not lose his resolve? This is a man who finds victory in defeat; life in death. Look at how Godly he is.

***

These series of talks on Islam, God-Centricity and Human Liberation were delivered with the aim of enlightening pious individuals of the function of religion in the attainment of the human purpose through our Earthly lives. Of necessity, our worldviews need to be broad and non-final in order to accommodate intellectual and moral evolution and the actualisation of our human potential. Such a worldview within religions is constructed through submission to God who is unending in all His beautiful facets whether as a creator or a moral agent. Furthermore, directed devotion to God brings about the truest sense of success since it allows humans to complete their humanness by becoming godly and godlike. In this respect religion through its practices, cultures and instructions has to be in sync with the human evolutionary existential condition. It must place God at the helm of human existence and be liberating. It has to empower human beings and instil confidence within them to take decisions and constantly learn through experience, mistakes and experiences. Present day Islamic theology and practices need to be weighed against the notions of God-Centricity and liberation so that they can be brought back to the their state of productivity and that they bring unity and spirituality within the Muslim community. God-willing the next series of talks will examine the basic underlying assumptions of Islamic theology and how an accurate appraisal of them can facilitate human growth and liberation.

Lightning Source UK Ltd.
Milton Keynes UK
UKHW040726050319
338500UK00001B/50/P

9 781999 862114